ALWAYS OUR CHILDREN

*One Mother's Unconditional Love
for Her Gay Children*

BY PAULA LEONETTE

StreamlinePUBLISHING

ALWAYS OUR CHILDREN
One Mother's Unconditional Love for Her Gay Children

Copyright © 2018 by Paula Leonette

9 8 7 6 5 4 3 2 1

First Edition

Printed in the United States of America.

ISBN 978-1-7325191-0-7

Library of Congress Control Number: 2018950173

Edited by Jeremy Jusek
Cover illustration by Trista Louise White
Design by Jane Toma

This book is dedicated with *unconditional* love to my husband and children.

You have made me stronger, better, and more fulfilled than I could have ever imagined. Your support, encouragement, and inspiration made it possible to write this book with enthusiasm and passion. This book is a sign of my love for you.

This book is also dedicated in memory of my father whose genuine love, affection, and encouragement will be forever in my heart.

To the LGBT community: May you always BE yourself, BELIEVE in yourself, LOVE yourself and SURROUND yourself with those who will love you *unconditionally.*

– Paula

"The way you view situations is key to creating a strategy for improvement."

- Oprah

Contents

Introduction

In March of 2013, more than two years before the United States Supreme Court legalized gay marriage, a heartwarming handwritten letter went viral to "Nate."[1] The letter was written by his father.[2]

> *Nate,*
> *I overheard your phone conversation with Mike last night about your plans to come out to me. The only thing I need you to plan is to bring home OJ and bread after class. We are out, like you now. I've known you were gay since you were six. I've loved you since you were born.*
> *- Dad*
> *PS. Your mom and I think you and Mike make a cute couple.*

This letter was posted on the Facebook page of FCKH8.com, an organization aimed at empowering youth through gay-positive shirts, videos, and activist campaigns. Founder Luke Montgomery stated the short letter was enough to inspire an online frenzy. His response was a major understatement: "so many people got excited about this posting." The letter to Nate was liked more than 70,000 times and shared more than 40,000.[2]

Nearly three years after federal law swung open the doors on marriage equality there are still a multitude of strained relationships between parents and gay children. The Supreme Court might have swayed judges on future rulings, but it definitely didn't sway all parents.

This is heartrending. What child doesn't want unconditional love from his or her parents? For some, unconditional love is a no-brainer and comes naturally. For others it may take time. Regardless, parents have to have their child's back no matter what!

I am not a psychologist or a psychiatrist. I do not claim to be Dr. Phil or Sigmund Freud. My last formal psychological education was in the 1970s when I took Psychology and Child Psychology courses in college during nursing school. Presently, I teach and coordinate a Nursing Assistant Program and one of my lectures is titled "Mental Health." That is where my psychological education begins and ends. I do, however, have expertise dealing with gay children. Of my five children, three are gay.

This book is my own "coming out". When I began to gather my thoughts and feelings in black and white format it became very clear as to why I am who I am and how I got here. As Oprah would say, it was an 'ah-ha!' moment for me. It is now very obvious that this journey led me to writing this book; a book to provide support for and give advice to parents of LGBT children. It may also assist parents of disabled, autistic, and handicapped children as well. In a world where parents demand perfection, sometimes it pays to remind ourselves that imperfections are equally beautiful.

The LGBT community is still underserved in our society due to misconceptions, fear, and bad advice. Families have been destroyed and gay people have completely walked away from faith and families, which are two very important contributors to the psychological health of children. Families, societies, workplaces, and churches are all guilty of oppressing the LGBT community thanks to ignorance and isolation. They need to be informed and reminded of the truth. They need to dig deep to understand. If the LGBT community was better understood, I truly believe the hurt, hate crimes, and misconceptions would vanish. As Ralph Waldo Emerson once said, "knowledge is the antidote to fear."

I am a mom who loves her children, unconditionally. As a result, this book was written from a place of passion, determination, and concern. I don't believe parents who scrutinize their children's sexuality don't love their children, but I do believe that love is too often conditional. An alarming 640,000 LGBT children under the age of 18 are homeless.[3] The upsetting statistics don't stop there:

> The study's other findings are equally bleak: 46 percent of homeless LGBT youths ran away because of family rejection of their sexual orientation or gender identity; 43 percent were forced out by parents, and 32 percent faced physical, emotional or sexual abuse at home.

...it's clear there are still problems in our society.

The wisdom and emotion I share with you stems from my experiences as a daughter, step-daughter, and most importantly, a MOM. I am excited and passionate about the journey we are about to take together. I don't want to change who you are. I just want to enhance who you are and what you know about our children.

My goals for this book are as follows:

- To connect with parents, families, and friends of the LGBT community
- To inspire and enrich the lives of those struggling with similar situations
- To be the instrument/tool that breathes energy and compassion into unyielding parents
- To be an inspiration to parents of LGBT children

I start with my personal experiences that I am certain molded me into who I am as a MOM. The positive and the negative experiences together definitely set me on a path of visionary searching that led to the kind of MOM I needed to be to support my own children. There were many powerful moments in my childhood that impacted me greatly and ultimately prepared me for my future role as a MOM.

I do not intend to hurt or shame anyone. *It is what it is* some might say. I plan to simply describe and define my visions, my perceptions, and my experiences. I need to share with you every step of the way throughout my "growing up" years. I need to lead you gently into the heart and soul of my coming out.

I included information in this book to assist parents struggling with their child's coming out. These guidelines and inspirational sources will hopefully improve your parent/child relationship regardless of your family dynamics. Why? Because only one response to a heartfelt coming out is needed. And that is love.

I am enthusiastic about my goal and vision to reach and energize you through this journey. Ralph Waldo Emerson said, "nothing great has ever been achieved without enthusiasm." I hope that my enthusiasm empowers me to embrace this mission and take you with me. Enjoyment of what you are doing combined with a goal and a vision equals enthusiasm. Together let us experience enthusiasm about our children. I want to assist you with understanding parenthood as it relates to LGBT children and who we really are as we live in this community of love. By writing this I hope to make this world a better place and share thoughts with you on unconditional love.

I may not be able to convince all parents to see things through my eyes and feel what my heart feels. I do hope that if I can contribute even a small piece of advice to assist you it might make the process easier. Overcoming and conquering negativity toward our LGBT children will speak volumes for better relationships, and ultimately make the world a better place.

CHAPTER 1

The Nature of Coming Out

I write "nature" because it is natural. Over the past twenty years, research has closed in on the biology and genetics that are responsible for same-sex attraction. After researchers at the University of California analyzed more than 140,000 regions of DNA they were ultimately able to predict a person's sexuality using only their genetic material.[4] Other studies have found the hormones that a fetus is exposed to in the womb play a role, too.[5] Additionally, brains in LGBT are wired in similar fashion, while straight brains are likewise similar to one another.[5]

Whether or not you believe the science (and you should!), please believe this irrefutable fact: If a child could make the pain of endless bullying and family ostracization disappear by changing their "choice," they would.

Acceptance is good. Once most people adjust to the reality of their child's sexual orientation they feel like they've had a whole new world opened to them. First, they become acquainted with a side of their child they never knew. They now are included in their child's life. As parents begin to meet others in the LGBT community they begin to recognize that these people are just like any other community. As a parent, you have to take care of yourself and your child. Reading this is your first step towards offering real support. You are showing him or her that you are open to new information and willing to become better-informed to help them through an ordeal society makes needlessly complicated. Supporting your child now should be a natural extension of your support as a parent.

Every child needs different things from his or her parents. It is up to you to learn how to communicate with him or her about their needs and issues surrounding sexuality. Some parents find that they are better able to understand and support their child by recognizing the similarities and differences in their own life experiences. In some cases it may help to talk about how you have dealt with hurtful incidents.

A flip side to this positivity is recognizing the realities of discrimination. You must recognize that discrimination based on sexual orientation is real, and the damage it does is hurtful in a unique way. Unless you, the parent, are also gay, there's little chance you really understand what they are going through. Here, you can support your child by educating yourself as thoroughly as possible about homosexuality. We need to help to bring it out of hiding in our society. It is the hiding that allows the prejudice and discrimination to survive.

As one mom said, "I reached a point when I was sad and confused, thinking what would I say when people asked, 'how are the kids?' And then it occurred to me that *they are fine*. I'm the one that's not okay."

I had to reach that point, too. And once I did, everything became easier. As we met our sons' friends and romantic interests, we found them to be wonderful people and realized that the LGBT community is terrific.

So what's the problem? The answer is society. When my husband and I realized society was conditioning us to cause unnecessary pain to our children we were able to refocus our efforts on interpreting society's rules in our own way.

Another parent once told me, "I would say that reading and learning more about sexual orientation is what helped me the most... laying to rest some of the myths that I heard. So the more I learned the angrier I got and the more I wanted to change society instead of changing my sons. For me it was my son saying to me, 'Mom I am the same person I was before!' Now I realize even more that really nothing has changed in his life. It was our perception of him, I guess."

I think the turning point for me was when I attended a local support group and began writing down my thoughts for this book. I was quick to realize that when most children and their parents accept their sexuality, they feel calmer, happier, and more confident. And of course that is what I wanted for my children. That is what all parents should want for their children. I did not want to be what was standing in the way of that, casting my oppressive shadow over my own kids' value of self-worth. I was teary eyed for many months off and on. I've always had a good relationship with my children. I don't think our children ever doubted our love for them.

But I do think that when I put in more effort, our relationships with our sons blossomed in a significant way. We have a bond simply because we know what they are up against in society. Regardless of how federal laws have shifted, there are still significant pockets of the country that don't understand.

It is really important to talk about it. It is important to know that you are not alone and that there are other people who have had the same experiences. It is possible to deal with your situation in a positive way, and prevent another disaffected child from become another homeless statistic.

And finally, good parents want to parent. Generally speaking, they don't want to be isolated from their child.

*   *   *   *   *

I want to make a difference!

The desire to inspire led me to researching this problem, conducting a survey, and spending enormous amounts of time immersed in the LGBT communities of Columbus, Ohio and Chicago, Illinois. I was determined to evaluate and analyze the way the LGBT community exists and survives its ups and downs. The LGBT community is a strong and close-knit group. They don't sell out their integrity and they don't settle for less. Through their wisdom I learned that there is nothing worse than betraying yourself, not being true to who you are, or being someone you are not and hiding the real you to make others feel more at ease. You should be able to come out loudly and proudly. When you try to protect your identity, you don't have spontaneity. You have filters in your head.

Having a head filter is an apt metaphor. Many LGBT feel like they're on a special watch 24/7, like spies operating in foreign territory. They do everything they can to avoid "giving themselves away," which is just a depressing way to say "being someone else for the benefits of others." This suppression leads to real, measurable problems. *Minority stress* is a condition experienced by disenfranchised groups within society: racial minorities, women, and especially LGBT.[6] Minority stress is directly linked to causing higher rates of heart problems and mental health issues in the LGBT community.[6]

What stands true and really sticks with me as well is: What you experience growing up stays with you forever. Whether it be rejection, neglect, and abandonment, or a loving and positive childhood, it all molds how we think, feel, and behave as adults.

I have looked into my siblings eyes on more than one occasion and still witness emptiness. We share that special history together that although was at times profoundly negative, it was something we faced together. We hold something in our hearts and minds that no one else can truly feel or understand. I love my siblings and hope that they can continue to find love and happiness through their present day family relationships. I hope for them that they have become better parents and spouses because of our experiences in our formative years.

*   *   *   *   *

We are a part of a greater plan and we have a role to play in that plan. Every step of the way we are unveiling coincidences as well as facing changes and uncertainty. Sometimes change can be negative and traumatic, yet these turning points can be the source of our life's journey and progress. For me, my children coming out was a major turning point. Perhaps not as significant as their own development, but significant nonetheless.

The point I'm making is that your children coming out will change you, too.

Sometimes I come to tears when I think of my sons and wonder if their lives have been a series of identity struggles and fears of rejection. Do they ever feel trapped in who they are, feel trapped in their personal self, feel incomplete versus feeling fulfilled? What about while they were growing up?

It saddens me to think of what they have faced. Our children need to feel secure, not threatened. They need a deep sense of fully being who they are, not feeling like an outcast or misfit. Minority stress literally shortens their lives, and lurking in the back of my mind is the fear that theirs have been stunted.

The fact is, people have rights and we need to protect them. We are all members of a great, big, human family and the foundation of freedom, justice, and peace in the world. It's the stuff strong communities are made of. We need to recognize the importance of inherent dignity and the importance of equal and inalienable rights for all.

Speaking with other parents I've learned that a common first reaction is "How will I ever handle this?" Most parents aren't prepared for the words "Mom, Dad, I'm gay." My husband and I, and other LGBT parents, most likely have gone through what you are now feeling. I can tell you with absolute certainty that you are not alone.

Gallup estimates that roughly 10% of adult Americans are gay.[7] While these numbers are contested plus or minus a few percentage points, what is true is that more Americans are feeling comfortable with coming out, albeit very slowly. From 2012 to 2016, the number of self-admitted LGBT rose from 3.5% to 4.1% of the population.[8] If that sounds like a small number, that 0.6% represents 1.75 more people who felt comfortable coming out in a four-year period.

It should come as no surprise that millennials feel more comfortable coming out than baby boomers, as the number of self-identified LGBT millennials rose from 5.8% to 7.3% within the same four-year period.[8]

Assuming the one-in-ten statistic is correct, and that each child-rearing family in the United States has an average of two children, then approximately one in five families has an immediate family member who is gay, lesbian, bisexual, or transgender. If you don't then you, unknowingly or not, have someone in your immediate social circle that is LGBT.

*   *   *   *   *

Who is this book for? The answer is that it's for everyone. It's for liberals in coastal cities, it's for the spiritually devout, it's for people who grew up in places filled with ideas about sexuality being a choice. It's for people who misinterpreted God's love as an instrument of oppression and conformity. It's for people who don't know where to turn when a lifetime of beliefs is broken by their children coming out, sowing confusion and discord in their response.

If this describes your situation, please know first and foremost: reach out to someone. There is power in reaching out. I can tell you from experience that talking really helps. There are books to read, telephone help lines to call and people to meet who, by sharing their own experiences, can help you move forward.

The second thing I can tell you is that, if you wish, you will emerge from this period with a stronger, closer relationship with your child than you have ever had before. That has been the case for me. However, do know you must make an effort, and the path can be difficult.

Some parents are able to take the news in stride. But many of us went through something similar to a grieving process with all the accompanying shock, denial, anger, guilt, and sense of loss. If you are dealing with those feelings, know that these are understandable gut reactions given our society's attitudes toward gays, lesbians, transgender and bisexuals. Don't condemn yourself for the emotions you feel. But please do focus. Remember what is important. Say the name of the child you've loved since birth—you owe it to him or her, and to yourself, to move toward acceptance, understanding, and support.

While it may feel as if you have lost your child, you haven't. Your child is the same person he or she was yesterday. The only thing you have lost is your own image of that child and the understanding you thought you had.

Think of it this way: imagine if you were taught all your life that a square has three sides and three points. So you draw this square over and over, only to get to art class and find out it's always been called a triangle. Now take this situation, complicate it with the love for your child, add in the shame of "what will the neighbors think!?" and you're getting close to how this process unfolds for some parents.

And if you think society isn't responsible for equating a coming out with loss, please know that while I was dealing with my own children's struggles, Democratic President Bill Clinton was telling soldiers to keep their mouths shut about being gay. "Don't ask, don't tell" was strict enforcement of oppression.

The loss can be very difficult, but that image can be happily replaced with a new and clearer understanding of your child. Instead of viewing this as loss, look at your child's coming out as opportunity. If your child is young, coming to an understanding with them is crucial to maintaining your bond with them going forward.

LGBT youth who are shut out by their parents have higher rates of suicide and substance abuse than their straight peers. Some LGBT teens protect themselves by putting as much distance between them and their parents as possible. If your son or daughter came out to you voluntarily, you're probably more than halfway there already because they cared enough to try to win over your acceptance. Your child's decision to be open and honest with you about something many in our society discourage took a tremendous amount of courage. It shows an equally tremendous amount of love, trust and commitment to their relationship with you. Now it is up to you to match your child's courage, commitment, trust and love with your own.

We think we know and understand our children from the day they are born. We are convinced that we know what's going on inside their heads. So when a child announces, "I am gay" and we hadn't a clue or we knew but denied it to ourselves—the reactions are often shock and disorientation. You have a dream … a vision of what your child will be, should be, or could be. It is a dream that is born of your own history of what you wanted for yourself growing up.

The apprehension you may feel is a product of our culture. Homophobia is too pervasive in our society to be banished from our consciousness. And, if you believe in God's presence in our lives as a commanding love for all His children, it is impossible to banish.

Many parents may confront a source of guilt. I've met extremely liberal parents with gay friends who were stunned to find themselves uncomfortable with their child's sexuality. These parents not only have to struggle with deep-rooted fears of homosexuality, but also have the added burden of thinking they shouldn't feel the way they do.

These parents intimated to me that it helps to concentrate on real concerns. The greatest question to ask is: what does your child needs most from you, right now? Try not to focus on the guilt. It is baseless and accomplishes nothing for yourself or your child. I speak from experience. For many years I lived with the guilt that I was somehow responsible.

＊   ＊   ＊   ＊   ＊

What is the best way for families to come out? Coming out is not an easy transition to make. LGBT children often feel fear regardless of how they assume their parents will respond. Some children try to protect us (or, in the more depressing cases, themselves) by avoiding the coming out process altogether.

The coming out process can be difficult for parents, too. Many, upon learning that their child is gay, respond poorly sending their kids right back into the closet. As they struggle with accepting their child's sexual orientation, they often worry about other people finding out. There is the challenge of fielding such questions such as "Has he got a girlfriend?" and "So when is she going to get married?"

Usually parents find that our fears are worse than reality. Some of us hold off for years in telling our own parents (our children's grandparents). Most grandparents figure it out before they are told, if that day ever arrives.

My advice to you is the same we give to LGBT individuals: Learn more about the changing attitude via medical, psychiatric, religious, professional, and political circles. There are plenty of authorities that can support the rights for the LGBT community. Statistics show that while many people are still in the closet, afraid of what coming out will mean, more and more LGBT feel confident enough to out themselves.

If you "know" your child is gay, prepare yourself for the coming out moment so you can make them feel as welcome as possible. Practice what you would say just like you would practice for a public speaking engagement or job interview. You want to be assertive since your image matters and it will relieve some of the nervousness. Say it with pride!

Yes, some people can be negative. You might get insensitive comments from relatives, friends, or coworkers. You will probably find that those comments are fewer than you fear. More importantly, you'll probably realize you don't care what they think.

Perhaps most importantly, remember that your child has been down this road already and **it is far worse for your child than it is for you.** This isn't about you. It never was. This book may be focused on you, but it's only focused on you so you can provide more support to a child that desperately needs it.

Your child may even be able to help. Remember, losing a few, judgmental friends is nothing compared to the pain of losing a child.

Please remember: who you tell about your child's sexuality should be a decision that *both* of you discuss and reach together.

*   *   *   *   *

In a world that still assumes all people are heterosexual, coming out is the only way LGBT people can make their sexual orientation known. And coming out is often considered a positive way to avoid societal invisibility that can lead to internalized self-hate or lack of self-esteem.

LGBT are often accused of "flaunting" their sexuality when they come out, when they are publicly affectionate with a same-sex partner, or when they wear gay symbols and t-shirts or participate in gay-pride parades. This is extremely unfair, especially when baseball games have "kiss-cam" moments, encouraging heterosexuals to kiss in public. The idea that LGBT shouldn't express affection is just an unfair mechanism designed to protect the general public from feeling uncomfortable.

You may be uncomfortable with your child's public displays of affection with his or her partner. Bear in mind that all couples, straight and gay, often show affection publicly because they feel love and appreciation for their partner. But stop and think: are you as uneasy about heterosexuals showing attention in public? In other circumstances, it may be a political decision to assert one's sexuality by wearing a t-shirt or participating in a public event. The only reason LGBT became a culture separate from the mainstream was because the mainstream ostracized them. If you worry about possible negative reactions to behavior that identifies your child as gay, keep in mind that some LGBT will censor their own behavior because they share those fears. But it is up to your child to make those decisions for themself.

Despite the fact that a significant portion of the population is gay, American society still prepares us only with heterosexual dreams for our children. The shock and disorientation you may feel is a natural part of a type of grieving process. You have lost something, your dream for your child. You also have lost the illusion that you can read your child's mind. Of course when you stop to think about it, this is true for all children, straight or gay. They are always surprising us. They don't marry who we might pick for them. They don't take the job we would have chosen. They don't live where we would like them to live.

Keep reminding yourself that your child hasn't changed. Your child is the same person that he or she was before you learned about his or her sexuality. **It is your dream, your expectations, and your vision that will have to change** if you are to really know and understand your loved one. Some parents feel they would have been happier not knowing about their child's sexuality. They look back on the times before they knew and remember this period as problem-free, overlooking the distance they often felt from their child during that time. If you remember that time as problem-free, keep in mind that your child probably remembers it as a dark time that they lived with a secret that made them feel ashamed and separate from their friends, parents, and community.

*   *   *   *   *

Sometimes coming out leads to strong denial. Parents sometimes react by rejecting what they hear. The most common refrains I heard were things like "It's just a phase, they will get over it" or "If you choose that lifestyle, I don't want to hear about it." These statements are natural, knee-jerk reactions, but I ask you this: What is so wrong with "That's nice honey, now what do you want for dinner?"

Pretending the problem doesn't exist is unhelpful. Denial and disapproval means you will *never* really know your child. A large part of your child's life will be a secret from you. You will never really know the whole person. It is important to accept and understand your child's sexuality because homosexuality and bisexuality are not a phase or a choice.

It is true some people experiment with their sexuality, trying to discover what is within themselves. However, someone who has reached the point of telling a parent that he or she is gay are no longer unsure or confused. By that point your child has given long and hard thought to understanding and acknowledging his or her sexual orientation. So if you are wondering if they're sure, please dismiss the thought. The answer will almost always be yes. Telling a parent that you think you are gay involves overcoming too many negative stereotypes and taking far too much risk for anyone to take that step lightly or prematurely.

Remember, the fact that they told you in the first place is a sign of his or her love and need for your support and understanding. It took a lot of courage. It also shows a very strong desire for an open, honest relationship with you. Reward that courage, because you'll be paid back with a stronger bond and more honesty than ever before.

Some parents take offense that their children took too long to tell them. These parents all fall under the same refrain: their child waited because of a lack of trust. For these parents, it can be painful to realize you didn't know your child as well as you thought. Please don't take offense. Remember the incredible pressure that society, and maybe even your community and social circle, puts on kids to conform. And if you can identify things you've said or did in the past that might have alienated their trust, recognize that their love and need for your support overcame their fears.

Parents may need time to process in their own "coming out process" in regard to their loved ones sexuality. We all have dreams for our children. This is not part of those dreams. This is not in the plan of life that you have for your child. There is no preparation for it. We all come from different walks of life yet what we have in common are similar feelings.

"Why us?"

"Did I go wrong somewhere?"

We worry about their future. But, we are also caught off-guard.

If you are caught off-guard, there are two things you should know. One, you should know it's okay to ask for a few minutes to process the information. And two, before you do walk away to process, you *need* to reaffirm your love and affection for your child. Make them feel loved first, then deal with your needs second.

*   *   *   *   *

Years ago, I truly believed that being gay was a choice. Like most parents in my area, I had a very limited understanding of what it meant to be gay. When I learned each time that one of my sons was gay, my head and thoughts felt frozen. My brain was in a state of strangeness and fog. I was scared. I feared for my children. I cried.

And running counter to all I've written to this point, I was not sad about their sexuality or personal troubles, but instead I was tormented by thoughts from people around me. I worried that not everyone would understand. I worried about friends, co-workers, and churchgoers. But more than anything I worried that my family, my siblings and father, would not love them. Time stopped in a way when the realization hit home. When I was alone I'd let loose the floodgates and cry. I wanted to know "why me?" I wanted deliverance. What I was getting wrong was my preoccupation with my own deliverance, which was overpowering my child's need for deliverance from his mother's judgment.

My son Anthony once said to me, "Being gay is not a choice, why would anyone want to choose to go through what gays go through?" I may not have fully understood at the time, but boy do I understand now. The worst kind of knowledge is the knowledge we acquire that is wrong and untrue. The fact is, some knowledge is just false, plain and simple. Part of maturing is relearning what is true.

We need to educate those that do not understand, because the alternative—losing the bond with our children—is unacceptable. We must stand with our children, always.

And that is the theme of this book, of my life, of the lives of the parents I've met. I've learned to embrace that most precious gift of all, my children. I was amazed as I began to jot down my feelings and emotions of my younger days. I quickly realized that I had serious issues with trust, relationships, and emotions. Looking closely at who I am and how I got here was a huge wakeup call for me.

In truth, I was facing for the first time who I was and why I am who I am. In many ways I'm an ordinary mom. Married with five children, RN at our nearby hospital, nurse instructor, ER nurse by trade, I always hoped to make a difference in the people's lives that I touched as a medical professional. Despite those lofty goals of helping others, it was years before I learned how to properly help my children.

The one thing that is extraordinary is that 3 out of 5 of my children are gay. All five of my children are good, kind, wholesome, and gentle. However, my three eldest sons have dealt with some extra difficulties in their lives that have shaped our entire family. So now, let me take you back to the beginning of this story. Let me tell you of my journey through a seemingly ordinary life and how I learned that accepting all of our children, regardless of orientation, was the right thing to do.

CHAPTER 2

Our Journey, My Childhood

My name is Paula. With this book I lay myself bare to tell all. I am not ashamed of who I am or of my children. Perhaps this message will help other parents reach a similar comfort level, allowing them to reconnect the love that may have been lost somewhere in the process of their child's coming out.

Perhaps this message will do something else: develop a new normal. A new normal for all LGBT families. A normal response by parents whose children are coming out. A new normal of acceptance and love for all.

I started this journal of love at age 56. Six years later, I invite you to join me on this journey of the last 62 years. Please, follow my footprints on the path of compassion.

✻   ✻   ✻   ✻   ✻

I was born on November 7, 1955. My name set the stage for my understanding of parent-child identity. From an early age I wondered if I was supposed to be "Paul Jr." I was the first-born and named after my dad, Paul. Did he hope for a son? What were his expectations of me as Paula? At any rate, I love my name and I am very proud of the legacy. I truly believe that giving me his name was the first of many ties that bonded my father and me.

My personality wasn't always this upbeat. My life was filled with lows, and it took a long-term concerted effort to round out who I am today. Today I feel positive, thankful, and forward-thinking about the past as well as the future.

I grew up in a dysfunctional Italian family. My parents divorced after 13 years of marriage that left behind four children. I was 11 when the divorce occurred. That was old enough for me to witness (and understand the consequences of) the deterioration of a marriage over a six month period, the result of an affair between my mother and my father's co-worker. My father, a well-known news reporter for a local TV station was successful and well-liked by the city of Cleveland, Ohio. He had solid bonds with law enforcement, lawyers, and judges in the Cleveland area. The affair left him emotionally destroyed—my mother fell in love with my dad's cameraman.

The divorce quickly divided the families in two. To a young, impressionable pre-teen, this event was, emotionally speaking, an earthquake. To this day, the aftershocks of this earthquake are still felt. My father gained full custody of us. For a father to gain full custody of his children in the 1960's was a rare court decision in those days, and probably spoke to his clout with members of the courts. Legally, the reasons for this decision were abandonment and neglect. For us, this decision was sad, scary and overwhelming.

Those days are foggy to me but I do remember the house suddenly feeling empty. The home changed quickly from a lively, happy environment to a cold series of rooms, devoid of furniture. The most striking detail I remember was her closets, standing empty, without her clothes and shoes. We four children were left distraught and numb, feeling as empty as the house and left in the care of our depressed and very bitter father. This was my crash course into rejection and low self-esteem. Later, when my first son approached me with his coming out, I felt transported back to that place of emptiness. I remembered thinking that no one could ever replace our mother and being frightened by this new normal.

In a way, I also thought it might be some kind of mistake, and any day I'd receive news that my parents would, in fact, be fine. When it was obvious that reconciliation was no longer an option for my parents, she vanished for good. Erased from our minds, she was not to be mentioned and, if we could help it, not to be remembered. It was as if she was a poison that needed to be discharged from our veins. As I write this 50-plus years later, tears still well up in my eyes and the frightened, panicked emotions return as if it were yesterday.

I have always said that children who witness divorce and the traumatic destruction of their family feel the impact on their lives forever. I very recently learned of a local 12-year-old that committed suicide. The suicide note that he left behind blamed his parents' divorce for his life-ending decision. Suicide seems like an impressively-permanent decision for a kid who is barely in his teenage years, but I understand completely. The impact of a broken family never goes away. It is a life-altering experience.

For us, the new normal in our household was *survival*. Dad would continue to report the news, keep us well-fed, clothed, and sheltered. With the assistance of my aunt, paternal grandparents, and occasional nannies we tried to recover and rebuild a family. My mother had moved to California with her new spouse and was not in any way a part of our new normal. Grandma, Aunt Helen, and I would try to replace the mom that no longer had a presence in her four children's lives, aged 3 to 11.

My three siblings and I were not quite a family but not quite foster kids, either. Our father loved us, but all feelings of home had vanished. I missed my mom and as time passed the emptiness in my heart didn't disappear. If anything, the empty feelings simply grew. A mother is a key figure in a child's life and glue to the family unit.

The divorce made me want to have children of my own. I wanted to be more successful than my parents were. I began to set my standards high for what was to be when I became a mom someday. This desire increased from a slow trickle to a gushing river the more I thought and prayed for a family. I was certain that I would always strive to be the best mom a child could ever hope for.

I'd hear comments that served to strengthen my steely resolve. Comments like "History repeats itself," "The apple never falls far from the tree," and "I hope you turn out better than your mom did" all cut deep into my fear of failing as a parent. I wanted to prove conventional wisdom wrong. Under these commitments I wrote a prayer to God in 1968. I was 13 at the time:

> *Please Lord, when I grow up, please make me the best mom ever. Please don't ever make my children wonder where I am or if I love them or not. Let my children know that I will be there for them and always love them.*

I did not see my mother again until I turned 18. I had a brief visit with her in California, and even that was tough to secretly arrange. I had told my father that I was visiting a friend in Florida while I made my real plans to head West. I arrived in California dismayed and scared, uncertain whether what I was doing was a good idea. What if she had left us behind because she really did not want us in her life? What if she sent me back home, or perhaps worse, notified my father before she sent me back home?

It didn't matter. I did not have enough time to get to know her again. I returned home after 24 hours, defeated and resolute in the truth: I didn't know who my mother was anymore. I was scared. She felt like a stranger to me. Was I supposed to stay in California until I discovered the depths of our relationship? There was so much time lost that building a bridge with her would take forever, I thought. I was also extremely nervous that my father would find out where I really went. Overpowered by the feeling that I was doing something wrong, I returned home quickly and so very confused.

In truth, the concept of "mother" was severely stress-tested in my 14th year. My dad had met a very ethnic Italian woman in her 40's. She'd never married, did not have children, and was living with her Italian-speaking parents and brother. Dad was very excited about his new relationship. He was convinced he found the new mom for his four children. The countless evenings that dad and I sat at the kitchen table as he cried over his failed marriage to my mother were fresh in my mind. I figured that this "new mom" would be better than no mom at all. This was, again, the new normal I'd have to live with.

Our step-mom entered our world and we couldn't help but notice dad's laughter and happiness returned. He even had more energy and time for us. He had peace of mind knowing that the replacement mom for his four foster children had completed the family unit. It was like our family had been restored.

Unfortunately this was not to be.

Just a few, quick months after she arrived I realized that this new mom would leave a bigger scar than the first. The new normal was not a feeling of abandonment. The new normal was a feeling of interference. I felt as if I was an obstacle between her and my father. I felt like a bother, a burden, a bad fit. I was her stepdaughter, not her daughter. And thus I learned the legacy of the name I shared with my father was not enough.

The house became a military compound in some ways. Not being allowed to sleep in on weekends, open the fridge without permission, or be a bother or burden to my stepmother was the careful path I was encouraged to follow. I was assigned to an overabundance of chores which I remember doing faithfully in hopes to please my stepmother and gain her love and approval. I was given a nickname by a relative around this time. I was called "Cinderella" in relationship to my ongoing assignment of chores. Although it was intended to be said in fun, it was repeated quite often. Deep inside this was another tug at my heart that would resurface as pain quite often. When I was not doing chores, I would hide silently in my room with my door closed to keep peace in our household and remain as obedient as possible. I often felt unwanted, rejected and a stranger in my own home.

My self-esteem quickly nosedived, too. I never felt I was good enough. My plans to be the best parent ever were shaken to their core, too. I felt like I'd never succeed at a mother-daughter relationship of my own that mattered.

The only maternal relationship I enjoyed was with our grandma, who did offer love and guidance. Unfortunately, this affection was too infrequent and she lived too far away for her to be of any regular comfort. Also, my mistrust of female blood bonds made her affection awkward and difficult to accept. I did not know how to receive love. Even amongst each other my siblings and I did not know how to express love or trust love. Somewhere along the way we lost the ability.

Even today, decades later, I am still trying to trust relationships and figure out what unconditional love is supposed to feel like. I do know that you need to have faith, patience, and trust to overcome rejection and to feel loved. Dad seemed happy as he continued to succeed in his career, leaving the duties of parenting to my new mother most of the time. If only she would not have reminded me so many times that she was not my mother. What appeared to be a resolution and a bandage for the open wound of divorce made me even more confused and wounded.

Rejection is such an ugly word. When rejected you feel as if you are not good enough. When rejected you are not accepted. Feeling rejected at any age or at any capacity can be a dangerous state of existence. *I am not your mother!* I can still hear this reminder in my ears that was repeated over and over again throughout my teenage years. I longed to be loved, hugged and accepted. I tried to analyze the situation the best I could to make sure that I could grasp what was happening in our family setting.

I tried to be understanding of her situation. I knew that marrying a divorced man with 4 children led to stressful life changes that she was unaccustomed to. Yet for me, I had a very difficult time adjusting and feeling accepted in the new family environment that was now developing as the new normal at our house.

The previously established routines of the household definitely created conflict. Before her arrival I was well-established as the commander of the household, helping dad facilitate chores and keeping a close eye on my younger siblings when he was at work. When she moved in we disagreed on how our home was managed day-to-day. My new mom quickly gave me the feeling that she had zero tolerance for me. I was demoted from commander to competition.

All the while I would continue my "Best Mom Ever" prayer. This was my mantra.

The rejection felt stronger to me when our stepbrother was born. Although my siblings were younger than me I suspect they may have felt the shift as well. The strict household rules continued. It seemed the affection was little and the rules were many.

Relief from rejection came on weekends when our stepmom and stepbrother would pack up and leave for her parents' house who lived several miles away. I often wondered if one of her weekends away would lead her to the final escape to freedom or would one of her weekends away make her realize that we were better together than apart. My father was quiet when she left, often distracted and withdrawn. It was then that I would seek attention and approval from my father that I so desperately craved.

As a teenager I was not rebellious. I did not turn to drugs or alcohol as an escape and I never tried to run away. I did not want to turn into an unruly teen and become a problem for my father. He seemed happy and I didn't want to rock the boat. I could not bear to see him regress back to his lonely and sad state that existed post-divorce years ago. I decided to accept the rejection as best I could and hope that someday I would win her acceptance.

I no longer cared about my well-being and felt there was no outlet for my problems. I experienced some very low times. I remember vaguely when, at 16 years old, I overdosed on medicine from the medicine cabinet. I wanted to die and put an end to rejection. I tried to commit suicide on February 14th. A cruel irony, since Valentine's Day is designated as a day of love.

It was a cry for attention. I wanted my father and step mother to recognize that many emotional needs were not being met. I had hoped the tragedy would somehow bring my stepmother and I closer. I truly longed for a solid and loving family unit especially for my siblings. After all, they were much younger than I and I thought they still had a chance to strengthen the family ties. I wanted them to be nurtured and loved.

The attempted suicide failed. It was obvious that God had better plans for me. I was starting to wonder just what those plans were. His plan, always a mystery, failed to reveal itself... however I never quit saying my custom prayer. Night after night, I prayed to be a better mom to my kids someday.

The overdose did not improve the family dynamics. Unsurprisingly, the event made matters worse. My stepmother made it very clear that she had little tolerance for the commotion caused by my attention-seeking behavior. This of course eliminated any hopes I had that she'd pity me or even tolerate me.

The rejection continued unabated and she became more distant with me. Only my father would attend my high school and college graduation. Even more difficult for me to grasp was his solo attendance for my wedding. The mother-daughter relationship I so longed for was obviously not going to be fulfilled as the "daughter." As a young adult my hopes turned to the future and I knew that someday I would fulfill this dream as the "mother" instead.

*　*　*　*　*

I sought out loving relationships in other ways. I admired my girlfriends who were close to their own mothers. I thought I wanted to become a teacher because I loved being with children. My high school friend had informed me that she was applying for Nursing School and would live on campus. We both agreed we would be great roommates. Susan, with whom I am still good friends with to this day, convinced me to join her at school. It was the perfect solution to remove myself from the dysfunctional mess I was in at home and it ultimately led me down a path of caring for others.

Once I became an RN, I quickly realized that I could make the biggest difference in someone's life in an Emergency Department. ER patients are most vulnerable, under great stress, often confused from feeling ill and medications, and perhaps more than anything else, desperate for compassion. ER nursing would allow me to make a difference every day in someone's life. I believed that this would be just what I needed to fit in. I learned even treating minor problems brought relief and established trusted bonds between myself and my patients. I quickly learned that the rewards are great when you offer compassion.

Years later, long after I'd entered the workforce, I'd use these experiences to try and attempt reconciliation with my stepmother. Unfortunately, the end result most often felt uncomfortable and awkward. When I did have my own kids, I often felt as if I suffocated my own children with love and attention to overcome the emptiness that I had experienced as a child. I overcompensated to make sure that my unconditional love for them was never doubted. My daughter once called it "smotherhood," which is perfectly fine, because I know from experience that's better than the alternative.

I cannot say how my parenting served to help or hurt my kids. They will be the judge of that. And hopefully, they will feel positively affected by my presence. I do know that I still have issues with trusting love, trusting relationships, as well as concerns over being rejected. I assume that these will always exist with me in some way. I will keep these in the back of my mind and continue this voyage.

So much of our childhood and family roots sets the tone for our entire adulthood, and informs our psychological development for the rest of our lives.

*   *   *   *   *

My brother, who is second-oldest, is a very quiet person. He tends to keep to himself and his family. He has a heart of gold and would help any-one and do anything for someone if they needed his assistance. In many ways he reflects all the positive aspects of our dad.

My next-oldest brother is also very private. It is sad to say that I do not know him very well. I've had only the occasional opportunity to visit and spend time with him. He does not have children, but he loves his many pets. I truly admire the unconditional love he showers on every cat and dog in his animal menagerie. He seeks rescues, trying to give abused ani-mals a loving home. I suspect the two of us have more in common than I know.

My sister embraces home. She does not travel much or go out much. I think this is because we lived without the comforts of home for so long. She seems less outwardly-affected by our childhood than the rest of us. Maybe it's because she knows how to shut down and avoid rejection. But only rejection. She has been a good aunt to my children, open, kind, and loving.

My step-brother has relocated to another state. He is married and I assume is living happily and comfortably. As we grew up together, we con-tinued to keep the peace and follow our father's requests to maintain a quiet and comfortable environment for all. I have minimal contact with him. Not long ago I was fortunate enough to have a long conversation with him to explain the history of me and my siblings. This offered tremendous closure for me, a healing if you will. He was never aware of our childhood history until recently. Whether it was well-received or not, honesty and genuine communication proves to me that they are important steps in maintaining solid relationships.

It is interesting to see the type of adults we have become. I can't imagine my children without a mom at age 3 (my sister), or ages 7 and 9 (my brothers). There were many emotions felt through all these years including resentment, rejection, tension, and loneliness. Despite this all happening fifty years ago, I still find there are aspects that are difficult to let go. And I still find these memories are shaping how I mature today. I constantly ask myself questions like: What have I learned? How can I rise above all this? Can I become a better parent? How can I use my childhood experiences to make my life and the life of those around me better? What was God's plan for me?

Luckily my children, nieces and nephews never faced rejection. Somehow we were able to search and find the genuine love for our children deep within our hearts despite our lack of experience with it. There is always hope to rebuild and replace lost or damaged love.

What I do know is my experiences are similar to those faced by LGBT individuals when they encounter rejection. They, as I did, feel lost without acceptance and love and the end result is emotional rot.

CHAPTER 3

Elements of Parenting

The plan God set out for me unfolded as I began to realize where my life was headed. There was much work left for me to do. By the time I was mid-career as an ER nurse I was grateful for my life. Grateful to have survived a drug overdose years ago. Grateful to have grown into an adult capable of mature emotions despite the truncated practice I'd had with my parents.

My suicide attempt formed my passion as a nurse, too. It became a very important mission to care for patients arriving in our ER due to an intentional overdose. I made it my goal to give them optimum medical care and assist them by talking and sharing my own story. I embraced the idea that if I could show these patients that I'd "been there," perhaps I could give them hope. I truly felt connected to these types of patients, because I felt like I knew exactly what they were missing. It was my intention to give hope, compassion, and insight. I knew that a person that intentionally overdosed must re-learn to love themselves again. They have to love who they are by cultivating self-worth and faith in their own faculties. If we do not believe in ourselves, we cannot expect others to believe in us. Caring for overdose patients meant more to me than IV therapy, pumping a stomach, and drug screening. I wanted, no, *needed* to give them hope. It was perhaps the first true sense of purpose I'd ever felt. As new normals go, it was definitely the most positive.

Another part of my new normal came in the form of Community Outreach Pediatric Nursing. I was asked to represent our hospital at area middle schools. It was identified that through our DARE program in the schools, a medical segment would benefit the young teens. I was extremely excited to take on this role. I accepted the position with a passion to make a difference in young lives, too, and prevent them from ever abusing drugs in the first place.

Since I took that role I have spoken to over 6,000 students in our county with three different presentations per school. The topics included tobacco, bullying, drugs, and alcohol. The drug presentation informed students of a typical ER visit in the event of an overdose situation. Although graphic and intense at times, I was convinced I was saving lives in the classroom. Helping children understand that they are loved beyond belief was all a part of my plan.

My most requested presentation was my talk on bullying. Bullying is extremely damaging to one's self worth. Bullying is a form of repeated physical, verbal, and sarcastic emotional ridicule. Belittling someone produces a toxic environment for the bullied. I have a fervent passion for this topic because I can relate to this painful and harmful behavior.

At the center of bullying are our nation's LGBT children and teens. LGBT individuals are at much, much higher risk for bullying. Research shows that LGBT teens are twice as likely to be bullied than heterosexual teens.[9] These numbers might be higher if more teens came out at a young age. More troubling is the suicide attempt disparity between heterosexual and LGBT teens: whereas 6% of heterosexuals attempt suicide early on, a whopping 29% of LGBT teens, almost a third, make the attempt.[10]

My sons faced bullying on several occasions. And of course, because kids can be cruel, my heterosexual children also faced ridicule because of their gay siblings. Who would've guessed that many years later I would be reaching out and educating middle school students about bullying at the very same school that my children attended years before? This is, after all, the great irony inherent in my life's plan. In loving my children, I was returning to a place they felt and experienced serious pain.

What many don't realize about LGBT is that they are simply people. Unique, wonderful, and special people. Good people. They are full of the same love, energy, and compassion as heterosexuals... if not perhaps more. By dealing with bullying and rejection, they learn how endearing those qualities really are, and how much this world desperately needs more of. So why do we make them feel as if they were misfits and don't belong? No one around me ever said it, but I truly believe that the world is a better place because of the LGBT community. Thus, by God, I have been chosen to educate and inform the world to better understand this.

This is the place for my Plan's prayer. It exhibits my newest mantra, designed to expand beyond my first prayer to encompass not only my kids, but rejected people of all persuasions:

*Let him show you how big His plan is, how wide and broad
His desire is to save everyone and save them completely. And
let Him make that transformation a reality in your own life.
Just as we celebrate the resurrection, let Him bury the old
you and raise a brand new life.*

Ten years ago I began a Nursing Assistant Program called Club Compassion, with the main goal of teaching good nursing care. I encourage and educate students not only to perform accurate nursing skills but to be compassionate. You truly cannot give good nursing care without compassion.

The foundations of my plan include certain elements that I believe acceptance of your children requires, regardless of the conflict between mother and child. The rest of this chapter is devoted to these fundamental elements that you will deal with as a parent of a LGBT child, and I hope by recognizing these elements, I can help guide all parents in their quest to love their children indiscriminately for who they are as people.

Compassion

This world would be a better place if we could all promote compassion with each other as part of our everyday lifestyle. How can we embed this in our daily routines? Staying present in the moment will help you lead a fulfilled life. The quality of our life is not dependent on the circumstances we encounter but what we learn from these encounters and how we react. In terms of compassion, I think it is helpful to choose a phrase and keep it in your heart. This is a simple way to remind us to live a compassionate lifestyle. My personal favorite, and the one that lives in my heart, is:

- *How you treat people defines who you are.*

Here are some others to ponder:
- *The journey matters as much as the destination.*
- *Be the change you wish to see in the world.*
- *Enjoy your popsicle before it melts.*
- *If you fly with the crows you die with the crows.*

- *Silence is violence.*
- *You may forget what I have said, forget what I have done, but I hope you will never forget how I made you feel.*
- *I make everywhere I go better because I was there. Practice that everyday.*
- *Strength does not come from physical capacity, it comes from an indomitable will.*
- *Stay connected to the world of the spirit.*
- *We are spiritual beings having a human experience.*
- *Live in the present moment, try not to dwell on the past, resist projecting the future, and feel the power of now.*
- *Live with compassion and love and good things will happen.*
- *Attention is the beginning of devotion.*
- *Look at everything and everyone longer and closer.*
- *I do not regret a single kind word or act from life but I regret the encouraging words I could have said but kept to myself.*
- *Know where you are going to land before you jump.*

MOTHERHOOD

My experiences as a mom were challenging but each child taught me how to be a better mom, which in turn made me a better woman, too. I showered them with love and affirmation in any way I could, as much as I could. Are my children happy? Do they know that I love them? Are they healthy? Do they know they're important? When I answer yes to all of these questions, life is good! I want my children to see positive images that reflect who they are. I want to change the view of LGBT individuals from taboo and controversial. I want to share and fill the world with a unique brand of beauty.

Of all the relationships we have in a lifetime, there is nothing quite like the one we have with our mother. Some lucky folks have always had wonderful and satisfying interactions with the person who gave birth to them. Others, unfortunately, have had to disinherit themselves for their own sanity. While it is hard to be objective about this most primal connection, it is safe to say that this relationship will color much of our adult behavior.

Back in 2004, my sons' sexuality was beginning to surface and I had feelings. They were mostly negative. Among them were fear, worry, inadequacy, paranoia, and confusion. Was it my fault they were gay? Did I do something wrong as they were growing up? Did I meet the needs of my children? *Should* I feel guilt? How did this happen? Is this God's plan? How will they be treated? Will my father and siblings accept and love them? Will people reject them? How will their father accept this?

As a nurse I had very real medical concerns, too. What about HIV/AIDS?

This question is relevant today, too. While AIDS initially spread fastest among gay and bisexual men, and drug users who shared needles, all people and communities now face the threat of AIDS. Therefore, every parent needs to be concerned about this disease whether your child is gay or straight. You should make sure your child understands how it is transmitted and how to protect him or herself.

Being HIV-positive or having AIDS carries a powerfully negative stigma. Not as negative as America in the 1980s, but negative nonetheless. Know that your child will need your support more than ever. You should also know that you are not alone. There are numerous local and national organizations that can help you with medical and psychological care. At this point, your relationship with your child can become even closer but your family will have to learn to adjust to the physical and emotional circumstances of your child's changing health.

COMMUNITY

"Whatever will the neighbors think?"

This is a very real concern. While it's easy to care more about your child, it's hard to discount neighbors entirely. This is especially true for families who consider themselves part of a close community or church.

We struggled with this. One of our neighbors had a difficult time giving their children permission to associate with one of our sons. Their son confided in our son that he was not permitted to have contact with him. The best you can do is be there for your child and assure them that the problem is with the other party's empathy, not them.

It's important to keep in mind that LGBT people come from families from all corners of the earth – from every culture, religion, ethnic group, and occupation. However, when society demonizes your situation, it's very easy to feel isolated. One parent once told me, "I thought I was the only mother in my town who had a lesbian daughter." At first I was startled. But then as I started speaking out on the issue, other parents started coming forward. And now every time someone says to me, "I need to talk with you," I know exactly what they want to chat about.

S O C I E T Y

Now that I'm in 2018 and my children are adults, I have come to a place of peace. I have always loved them unconditionally. I understand their situations better.

What a difference the last 20 years has made! It helps that society is becoming more accepting. I had fear that my sons would be judged and viewed negatively throughout their entire lives. I understood rejection well and I did not want the same for my sons. I thought my sons would be viewed as a disease, not a person. How would they find pure happiness if they were viewed in that light?

I worried about abuse and bullying. I could not bear the thought of someone hurting them just because they were gay. So I cried, I worried, I prayed, and I loved.

It is sad to think that during their teenage years they probably experienced many, many times where they were forced to put on a false appearance because of who they were expected to be. It is sad to think that there are so many people out there that marry and settle down and fight the inner battle within themselves because they are afraid of others' perceptions. You just want your children to be happy and to be in a place of acceptance and happiness. How tortured my sons must have felt during their teens.

Nobody wants their children to struggle deeply. Blaming others, even if at fault, will not get you closer to your goal. (Parents, don't blame yourselves or your kids, hint hint!) Keep moving and reorient yourself and start fresh. Think positive and think love! Find inner peace because life can be incredibly confusing and difficult. We wonder why uncertainty and pain happens to good people. It's a mystery and outside of our control. Heaven does things sometimes to attract strong attention. Sometimes we need to have patience, confidence, and trust that everything will work out for the best if we give it time and faith. Try to refocus, this is not about the sex, it is about falling in love. Everyone should be able to fall in love in the way it is suitable for them.

When you have to make a tough decision you face a crossroad in your life. Crossroads represent change and change produces uncertain times about the future. Look for special clues and hints when you are at the point of major change. Sometimes these changes are life changing in a positive way that isn't, at first, easily noticeable.

THE COSMOS

Advice is very much a fundamental element of parenting. So many parents ask "Why is my child gay?" If you don't believe in the scientific reasons, this is going to be an extremely challenging question to answer.

Yet most parents aren't questioning the science, instead they're asking this to the cosmos. It's asked semi-rhetorically, and it's asked for a number of reasons. They may be grieving over losing an image of their child. They feel they did something wrong. Sometimes they feel that someone may have lured their child into homosexuality. Finally, some wonder if there is a biological cause of homosexuality, and if it was their own genes that "corrupted" their kid.

One response is to wonder "How could she/he do this to me?" This is perhaps a selfish reaction, but it should be recognized as a human response to pain. We turn to this reaction when we are grieving, and this question is symptomatic of a parent grieving over losing an image of their child. As you work through your feelings you may discover that the only thing your child has done is to trust that your relationship could grow as a result of you knowing the truth about their sexuality.

You may feel that your child has been led into homosexuality by someone else. It is a popular misconception that the LGBT community recruits members. The truth is that no one made your child LGBT. He or she most likely has known that he or she was different for a very long time.

Other parents feel that their parenting is the cause of their child's sexual identity. This is the theory that I had adopted. For years, psychology and psychiatry have banded around theories that homosexuality is caused by parental personality types like the dominant female, the weak male, or perhaps by an absence of same-gender role models. These theories, decades obsolete, are no longer accepted by the medical community.

Gay people come from all types of families. Some have dominant mothers while others may have dominant fathers. Gay men, lesbians and bisexuals are only children, youngest, middle, and oldest children. They come from families with siblings who are gay and families with siblings who are not gay. Many come from what society would consider "model" families. Many parents wonder if there is a genetic or biological basis to homosexuality. Science may not have definitively proven the exact causes of sexual preferences, but what science has done is proved beyond all reasonable doubt—through brain scans, neural network maps, and genetic research—that homosexuality is due to different chemical makeups in the brain, not choice.[5]

ADVICE

I have put together a list of points made possible through collaboration with the help of my LGBT children, as well as friends from Chicago and Columbus:

- *Seek meaning, not approval.*
- *Don't chase recognition.*
- *Find the people who really love you.*
- *Enjoy simple things and simple pleasures.*
- *Embrace what you love.*
- *Self-acceptance is key.*
- *Live your life's purpose enthusiastically.*
- *Respect feelings.*
- *You have to be true to who you are.*
- *Spend time with people who really love you.*
- *Know that everyone has their own strengths.*
- *Breakdown personal boundaries to pursue your dreams and to find happiness.*
- *Find your inner self to mine the strength and endurance needed to survive tough times. Be proud of who you are. Allow those around you to see the goodness.*
- *Move through your fear; we can control our mindset.*

FEAR

Don't hold back because you are afraid or because you have been hurt. Acknowledge your fear, accept it and get past it with confidence. You can't change the past, but what you can do is remove what hurts so it will not have the power to continue to cause you pain. Pain continues to follow you if you don't release it.

Don't smile through the pain! It is good to let things out, detox, then move forward from there. And finally, I hope you will keep a positive attitude, love yourself, and have faith. Head in the direction that you believe to be your destiny. Open your mind to your own potential to fulfill your destiny. Stay alert to the signs for your perfect mate. And know your strengths and use them to your advantage and shine!

Remember, knowledge is the light that vanquishes fear.

THE NATURE OF HOMOSEXUALITY

Homosexuality is a normal variation of human sexuality. Using the words perversion, sickness, and abnormality is not only medically incorrect but it is very hurtful to those targeted. LGBT people are expressing sexuality that is normal and natural to them. For them to express sexuality in an opposite sex relationship is unnatural and abnormal to their brain, and their brain dictates their behavior.

Don't condemn yourself for the emotions you feel. But, if those feelings are profoundly negative, you cannot take those feelings out on your children. You owe it to him or her, and yourself, to move past possible feelings about immorality and toward acceptance, understanding and support.

While it may feel as if you have lost your child, you have not. Your child is the same person that he or she was yesterday. The only thing you have lost is your own image of that child and the understanding you thought you had. That loss can be very difficult, but that image can happily be replaced with a new and clearer understanding of your child. If your child is young, coming to an understanding with him or her may be crucial.

THE POSITIVES

I can tell you that there are many plusses once your child comes out to you.

For instance, you will begin to recognize what an incredible child you have that he or she wants to share this with you, and so completely wants you to be a part of their lives. Look at the trust that has been placed in your hands and the guts it took to do that. To some extent, this is true in all parenting relationships – whether the child is gay or straight, but the walls society places around any deviation from normal sexuality heightens this trust's importance.

There's a necessary separation between parent and child as the child moves toward adulthood. Your child may reach conclusions you would not have reached and would do it without consulting you. In this case, it is particularly difficult because the conclusion your child has reached is important and often unexpected. You may have been shut out of your child's thinking for a long period of time. LGBT individuals may hold back from their parents as long as possible because it has taken them a long time to figure out what they're feeling about themselves. In other words, LGBT youth often recognize at an early age that they feel different but it may take years before they can put a name to those feelings.

Because we still live in a society that misunderstands or is fearful of the LGBT community, it takes time for them to acknowledge their sexuality to themselves, and even longer to acknowledge it to others. LGBT have often internalized self-hate or insecurity about their sexual identity. It may take time for someone to think through and work up courage to tell a parent. Even if you feel your child should've known they could tell you anything, remember our culture's treatment of the LGBT. Remember Bill Clinton's "Don't ask, don't tell" rule.

So even as you may grieve for not having been able to help your child through that period, or even if you believe the outcome would have been different if you had been involved earlier, understand that your child probably could not have told you sooner. If you believe in God's plan, believe that this moment was chosen for a reason. Most importantly, recognize that the coming out moment is an invitation to a more open and honest relationship. The defining trait that should come from a parent-child relationship should be love-infusing and more.

In Conclusion

Parents, to sum it all up:

- *Have an alert presence in your child's life.*
- *What really matters in a child's life is love, health, and nurturing.*
- *Care about who they are, even if you don't understand who they are.*
- *Rejection is damaging.*
- *Appreciation and praise have great results.*
- *Children are the products of their parents; you become the person that revolves around your childhood experiences and it structures your adulthood.*
- *Love your children for who they are.*
- *Let go and release your unhappiness with the situation.*
- *Have faith and patience.*
- *Don't be afraid to fail.*
- *We need to stand together!*

Attitudes toward the LGBT community have started to change in our society. They are changing relatively quickly. Will our children be discriminated against? Will they have trouble finding a job? Will they be physically attacked?

Or, if you are a parent suspicious of your child's coming out, ask yourself this: at a time when people are recognizing the LGBT conditions for what they are—vulnerable, distinctly human, and scientifically confirmed—do you really want to be on the wrong side of history?

There are many places now where our children can live and work relatively free of discrimination. Many cities, towns and states have worked towards recognizing homosexuality as natural. These jurisdictions have taken measures to ensure non-discrimination.

These are positive signs, but I wouldn't have bothered with this book if I thought society was "fixed." It's not. We still have a long way to go. Please recognize how important your child's coming out is, and recognize these core aspects of being LGBT in our society. With peace, love, and understanding, you can make this one of the best moments in your child's life.

CHAPTER 4

My Children

LOUIE

Louie is our first born.

My husband and I wanted a boy first and our wish came true. He was very easy to raise, stayed out of trouble, very domestic and was always a big help to me. He has always been respectful and kind. He was and still is an amazing older brother to his siblings.

Louie hung out with numerous girls in high school and very few guy friends as I recall. The day he moved out of the house to his own place at age 20 was the day I found out he was gay. I had no idea and honestly I did not believe it.

While still living at home, I remember that he came home after going out one evening with facial bruises and a concussion. He never told me that it was a hate crime because of his sexual orientation. That realization came to me after I learned he was gay. The fear and anxiety took much longer to repair than the physical injuries. I truly cannot remember the exact words he used to tell us that he was gay but I do remember how I reacted. To this day, I am ashamed of my behavior.

I yelled at him and lectured him. I told him that he had to change immediately. I told him he needed to "talk himself out of being gay." I told him he was "making a big mistake." I remember that he apologized for disappointing me and asked me not to be mad at him. He was terrified. His face was awash in anguish and betrayal.

Meanwhile, I was ignorant and frightened and, most of all, in shock. I remember how he held his head down looking at the floor. He would not make eye contact with me. To this day, I wish I could erase what I said to my son. I should have been supportive and loving that day but I wasn't even close.

Today, I am so very proud of him as he has reached his career goals and followed his dreams. He is such a good son and has an amazing partner that we love and adore. He is happy and he is healthy. I am so happy that he lives nearby. What more can a mother ask for?

P A U L

My second son, Paul the comedian, definitely mastered humor therapy. Humor improves morale, decreases stress and makes good things happen. He is a people person with a figurative million friends. Everyone that knows Paul loves him dearly. He's a pleasure to be around, charming and electric. People often quip that Paul is "sunshine, no matter the weather outside."

Paul's coming out was another shock to me because he was active in sports during high school, very athletic, and adored by girls. I guess at that time I did not think someone gay could also be a football, baseball, and wrestling star. He had the same girlfriend all through high school and they were always together. He was tough and not afraid to speak his mind. These qualities, combined with his relaxed, easygoing nature, made him popular and confident. I always believed Paul's motto was "better to ask forgiveness than permission." If he wanted to do something he just did it.

Sometime between high school graduation and college I started getting the vibes that he was gay. I don't remember any specific day that he came out to us. He just didn't bother to hide it.

Presently he is happy and healthy, living in Columbus, Ohio. His father and I have spent many weekends getting to know his friends in the North High Street area. He is engaged to his partner, Benjamin and we couldn't be happier with his choice. Many years ago, I would have never dreamed that I would be hoping and praying that each of our sons would find a male significant other that would make them happy and enhance their lives. Yet here we are, absolutely overjoyed to have Benjamin in our family. It is his new normal, and it brings all of us the greatest joy I could've ever imagined. Their wedding date is set for September 29th of this year, 2018.

And I couldn't be happier to be a part.

ANTHONY

My third son Anthony was the most open of the three boys and the most obvious to me. He kept himself active in high school with the Gay-Straight Alliance. He was bullied and ridiculed for his openness, yet his courage was absolute. Bullying never deterred him from supporting the cause.

You'd think that by Anthony I'd be a pro at the coming out process, but truthfully, at the time, it wasn't easier for me. Each time I learned that a son was gay, I needed time to absorb it and think it through. Each time I questioned why it was happening. I wondered if it was something I did during pregnancy or as our children grew up. In fact, having three gay sons made me think it was my fault *even more*.

One step at a time, that's all I could do to try and grasp the plan. I knew by Anthony that I had to keep moving forward, embrace them, and love them even though it seemed so challenging for all of us. I kept telling myself that I needed to be thankful for what I had and continue to cherish my children in the most positive way possible.

Anthony had a serious health issue at age 13. I still remember the evening before his 10-hour surgery when my husband and I were told that his life was threatened by his condition. When I look back at those frightening days during the surgery and his critical recovery, I recognize those moments as a huge wake-up call for me. If I had a coming out moment of my own, that would be it.

I am just so grateful that he is alive and well. To have him on this Earth with good health and well-being is the real blessing. Gay or straight, the fact that he is with us today is the greatest gift a parent could hope for. I have to imagine that the worst pain anyone could ever feel is the pain of losing a child.

Anthony in particular is easiest to talk to about being gay and remains open and supportive in his quest to help us understand both him and his brothers. I truly believe that his sexuality, the bullying, the traumatic surgery, and the medical issues post-surgery all led him towards his career path in child psychology. He is making a difference in children's lives, one child at a time, and we are very proud of him.

Anthony moved to Chicago to find diversity, as he told us. Presently, he does not have a significant other but did have a long term relationship that we are hoping will continue as a solid friendship between them. We have become quite fond of this gentlemen and we have grown a love for him as if he has always been a family member.

My sons have been the great inspiration for me to write my book. Leaving Chicago/Columbus or heading to Chicago/Columbus has always been the perfect time to jot down thoughts and information about each trip and how it has improved my understanding of the LGBT experience.

JOSEPH & NICOLE

Our two youngest are not gay, but I'd be kidding if I suggested they didn't teach me about compassion, either.

Our youngest son is a college graduate with a Master's Degree in sports management. He is settling into adulthood and has a strong and long time relationship with his girlfriend. He lives nearby and has always maintained such a closeness with his father and grandfather. We are so very proud of him. He was faced with ongoing bullying all through high school, not because he was gay but because he had gay brothers.

Our daughter just graduated from CSU with an MBA. She is the toughest of the bunch. I suppose being the youngest of five and having 4 older brothers is a solid recipe for toughness. She faced many episodes of defending her brothers when bullied. This also was the tool that molded her strength and toughness. Most know her as a smart and amazing individual once they learn who she really is.

*   *   *   *   *

I often wondered why I did not fit with the high school moms. I did not have many friends as my teens attended middle and high school. I volunteered for certain events and groups, yet I was rarely asked to join or participate. It occurred to me much later that perhaps this was because our family was different than the norm. Our normal wasn't their normal.

Of course, there is the possibility I was being paranoid and perhaps they just had enough mom volunteers for their events. *Perhaps.*

In Memorium

There are parents all over the world who have not been as fortunate as us. Many parents have lost children to illness or accidents. My husband and I learned very quickly how precious our children are to us and how quickly we could have lost Anthony to an illness. Life is so precious. Thus, I am dedicating this section to the memory of these special *Angels in Heaven* that I have known in some way. They will never be forgotten:

Dominic DeFranco	Scott Poley
Carolina Del Val Saenz	Lucas Reichert
Brittany Flowers	Logan Sambula
Anisha Moana Hull	Leslee Sciria
Riley Kenneley	Dylan Sheneman
Anthony McGill	Amanda Todd
Michele Monastero	Gino Zavarella
Jerrilyn Montgomery	

The Yin and Yang of Our Children

There is negativity in denial. There is positivity in acceptance. Our family's story includes both. Here is what I learned about both.

NEGATIVITY

Any negative emotion that is not fully faced and seen for what it is the moment it arrives does not disappear completely. Your brain has a very effective defense mechanism: it chooses not to feel it at all, blocking it. This traps it in our body and soul forever. This negative emotion never fully faced festers, manifesting rising internal stress until it can create psychological scars. This is a dangerous and harmful state of being. This state of being is what leads to an addiction of unhappiness, and worse. Some people allow their negative emotions to feed on their positive emotions.. A person trapped in this cycle immediately jumps to negative conclusions, and unhappiness becomes their disease. Nothing good comes from negative energy.

Fighting the negativity is tough. You must know yourself well and determine what your true needs are. You must keep what matters to you and your life in perspective. You know who you are by your actions and reactions. You know what is most important to you. How you react to people and situations, especially when challenged, is the best indicator of who you are and how well you know yourself.

In addition, knowing who you are *not* is a great tool to knowing who you *are*. Acknowledging the good in your life also identifies who you are and is the foundation for learning who you are. If you give compassion you will receive it. You cannot receive what you don't give. If you act in a loving way toward all living things, compassion will always turn things around. Expressing kindness, consideration and the desire to help is what compassion consists of. Be enthusiastic. Nothing clarifies the value of life more than having compassion and positive energy to balance every day and every worthwhile relationship.

If my children are healthy, happy, and being true to themselves then I know everything will be okay. Men and women's choices, behaviors, and attitudes should not be judged as "normal or abnormal." These behaviors and choices should not be subjected to verbal or physical abuse from anyone. Life is about happiness, health, and wellness.

Knowing this, we should focus on the positives: walk barefoot in the grass; just breathe; checkout more sunsets; smell the trees, grass, and fall leaves; and after a steady rain observe the luminescence around you. Soak in the gift of traditions and collect wonderful memories together. Family celebrations, Thanksgiving, and more contribute so much to our wellness. We often overlook the simple gifts given to us that surround us each day. These sound like an assortment of platitudes crunched together, but to a great extent they are true. Being able to stop and smell the gardenias is a key component to keeping the demons at bay.

All of us are unique and different, not just the LGBT. We each have uniqueness and we are all endowed with gifts. We may not see this at first, especially if we are exerting all our energy trying to fit in. In other words, trying to be something we are not.

We may have a different walk or talk, a different way of learning, a physical appearance that doesn't match others expectations, or a different way of expressing ourselves. We need to celebrate this uniqueness. Cherish who you are as a person and act out and do things out of love and compassion. Every day should count. Every day should matter. Those that we love should know that and be aware of that love every day. We are all sexual beings; we all struggle with desires, loneliness, identity and orientation. We have more in common than what divides us. We should support and respect every human person.

After all, when we die, the only thing that really mattered is how we treated each other. Live with compassion. Silence is violence—when we refuse to tell the stories of the people we love, and who love us, we actually participate in their oppression.

The manner in which LGBT people live their lives, not lifestyles, is as varied as the manner in which heterosexual people live their lives. LGBT people have lives, not lifestyles. Please don't refer to your child's behavior as "the gay lifestyle."

POSITIVITY

We have been very fortunate to visit Chicago on numerous occasions to share wonderful times with many of Anthony's friends in the gay community. Our son is always very excited for us to meet them. We have spent many visits in or near Boystown, Halstead and other LGBT communities. I believe that we represent "parents" as a collective whole. Our presence sends a message to them as parents, that we do care, and we respect, love, and accept who they are.

These communities are lively and friendly. It is wonderful to watch them let their guard down and relax. I particularly recall visiting a gay establishment, Buck's Bar where I felt like a rockstar whenever I visited. Many knew who we were and things about our lives. One man thanked us for being present at the bar with our son. Another man stated, "You are a real trooper to be hanging out with us," as if they were contagious. So many men came up to my husband and me to chat or just to welcome us. They seemed very surprised that we would want to spend time visiting a gay bar.

Quite frankly, it was wonderful. The atmosphere was lively, friendly, and energetic. There was no negativity or arguing... it was mostly hugging. At one point, I looked across the table at my son and saw that little boy again. Blond, curly hair, with an infectious smile and it brought tears to my eyes. There would never be a moment in time that I would want him to doubt my love or feel rejected by me. I commented on the amazing atmosphere and he replied, "Mom, we have all been through so much as gay men. We have dealt with unkindness and bullying. We are relieved to be in an environment that is accepting and caring."

I learned some of them have no contact with their families because they are not accepted. Some have been assaulted, bullied, or harassed in public, at work and even home. Some have been told not to visit during the holidays because certain relatives would be uncomfortable. Yet, as we visit these men, my husband and I felt nothing but an acceptance and compassion, despite their harsh histories.

There is definitely a sense of unity, trust, friendship between them.

It was at Buck's Bar where I observed and absorbed so many feelings and words. It was at Buck's Bar that I developed a strong desire to write a book about how I was feeling and what I was seeing. I was starting to understand the gay community much better. I will be first to admit, I love going to gay bars.

Each time I visit Chicago or Columbus it is difficult to leave. I look forward to every visit. As I drive away, I am near tears. I leave Chicago/Columbus every time in the same state of mind. I hate to leave them so far from home, hoping they are happy and safe. Because they are gay it makes me worry more. I find comfort in knowing that they have a strong friendship base. I am grateful that they surround themselves with good people.

That unity and friendship is the one component that does make it a bit easier to leave for home each time. I know that they are in a good place because of their network. It is hard to describe the warmth and closeness that I feel when sharing time in these communities, but it's clearly due to their standing united against society's more sinister impulses.

I feel this camaraderie in my heart. There I have so much love for my children, and the feeling is so incredibly strong. I feel the same way when I leave Paul in Columbus after visiting him. Each departure is bittersweet. I know they are living in gay-friendly cities, and that makes life easier for them. I know that this is where they feel a sense of belonging and comfort.

The last thing I'd like to share is a note from Anthony that we received a few days after visiting Chicago:

Dear Mom and Dad,

I had a wonderful time with you both and the family this weekend. The dinner and family time was a lot of fun and I am so lucky to have you both as my parents. Your love and support is what makes me want to do well in life and pursue my goals. Thank you so much for the groceries and gift card and most importantly your love.

Love,
Me

...NOW THAT'S WHAT IT'S ALL ABOUT!!!

(1) Lou, Paula and baby Louie; (2) baby Louie; (3) Lou with baby Paul and Louie; (4) Louie and Paul; (5) Paul

(6) Anthony and Joey; (7) Anthony; (8) Lou, Paula and the boys;
(9) Leonette Family: Louie, Joey, Lou, Paul, Paula, Joey and Nicole.
(10) Joey; (11) Nicole and Paula

(12) Anthony, Louie, Nicole, Joey, and Paul; (13) Papa and Louie;
(14) Louie and Nicole; (15) Anthony and Lou; (16) Anthony, Joey, Paul, and Nicole;
(17) Paul; (18) Lou and Joey; (19) Nicole and Paula; (20) Paula and Paul;
(21) Joey and Anthony

(22) Nicole and Papa; (23) Joey;
(24) Joey, Nicole, Anthony, Louie, Lou, Paula, and Paul; (25) Joey and Paula;
(26) Lou and Nicole; (27) Anthony, Nicole, and Louie; (28) Papa and Anthony;

*(29) Anthony and Paula; (30) Nicole and Louie; (31) Nicole and Joey;
(32) Desiree and Joey; (33) Anthony and Paul; (34) Lou, Paula, Joey and Nicole;
(35) Nicole and Kyle; (36) Desiree, Joey and Stella*

(37) Paula and Louie; (38) Paul and Benjamin; (39) Paul, Paula and Lou
(40) Joey, Paul, Nicole, Louie, Anthony, Lou and Paula;
(41) Hadley, Anthony, Lou and Paula

(42-44) Pride Parade – Columbus, Ohio

CHAPTER 5

Community Support

I did not openly advertise my status in the past, but tried not to deny it either. Until publishing this book, I have always been very selective of whom I shared my family story with. I always feared that some would not understand how blessed my family dynamics really are. I still feel the need to protect my children from the negativity and rejection if I sense it in the air. They are *always our children* and they are the most cherished gifts of all.

I am certain that our experiences aren't unique. Many gay children are likely facing some of the same experiences I faced in my divorced and abusive step-parent atmosphere. When analyzing my childhood years against that of my kids', I realize that I began to create a therapy of my own to cope. My therapeutic goal was to put conflict to rest. A bittersweet reflection on the beauty and agony of loving and understanding your children no matter who they are. It is a personal thing. Just like my daughter's *smotherhood* dubbing, I am no doubt finding my interest in the LGBT cause therapeutic.

As I interpret the pain, beauty, and the wonder of growing up, I am hoping that I can change perceptions in the way parents perceive gay life. You have to reach out in the community (Find your own Buck's!) to help them feel they are not alone or disconnected. They should not feel that their lives exist on the fringes of society because of their sexual orientation. This was very clear when visiting Union in Columbus and Buck's in Chicago.

What I know for sure is that because of my gay sons, I have learned a lot about life. You have to be who you are and own it with grace. No matter what the day looks like... embrace it. You don't get another chance at living. Life is a gift, be grateful for the things that make you laugh, smile, and keep us enriched in who we are. Appreciate the little stuff! Laugh!

Now, much of this positivity was *years* in the making. I did not get to this point in my life without help. This chapter is dedicated to the support group I discovered while trying to understand my sons' orientations. Before I re-visit those experiences, I have two messages I'd like to send. The first is to gay families as a whole, and the second is to parents of outed gay children.

> *To Gay Families,*
>
> *I hope you would have a vision and focus on that vision.*
>
> *Stay on track and focus on what makes you a happy family. It is okay to be different and give yourself permission to be different so you remain true to yourself. Begin where you are and do what you can to understand one another. PUSH!!*
>
> *You can do this! You can embrace your relationship if everyone tries.*

> *To Parents,*
>
> *We need to accept that while life is a mystery, we all have a role in it as the mystery unfolds. We need to act on our dreams and be present to the appearance of the divine in our day-to-day existence. That is our destiny.*
>
> *Flexibility is key. If your child loved you enough to tell you they are LGBT then love them strongly and help make this world a better place for all that are LGBT. The best things take effort. We have convinced our generation that if you are good at something, it must be effortless.*
>
> *I have found that the opposite is true. The best work is labor-intensive. When you reach the top of the mountain you will experience reward, rejuvenation, and relief that much has been accomplished. Have strength and give much effort to get to know your LGBT child for who they really are. Acknowledge them and accept them. Work hard at appreciating who they really are as a person. Care about who they are even if you don't fully understand.*
>
> *That is your job as a parent!*

My journey to make a difference in the lives of the LGBT community began with the support group I joined. I became educated and relieved once I started attending the support group meetings. This was another *Ah-ha!* moment for me; another piece to the puzzle that taught me about the bigger picture. We were a group of parents with LGBT children. Comprised of more moms than dads, approximately 20-30 people attended each meeting. Visiting my sons and learning about their friends taught me about their perspective. The missing puzzle piece that the support groups offered was the perspectives of other parents.

As parents, we had this secret amongst us and for various reasons couldn't talk to anyone about it. At the support groups we could be open and honest. It was here that I would tearfully announce to the group that I had three gay sons. It was here that I would tell them that I believed it was my fault that they were gay. I wasn't sure what I could have done but, at the time, I was still convinced it was my fault.

I did not know that a support group existed nearby, and actually I stumbled upon it quite by accident. I love Sundays and I enjoy mass. My husband and I developed many good friendships within our church family. I love having Sunday off, which always gave me a break from being on duty as a nurse and a guaranteed pasta dinner with the family.

I decided that I wanted to become more involved in my church, and maybe give something back. I was looking for opportunities to involve myself via the flyers our church puts on the community bulletin board. My eyes stopped at a trifold flyer with a rainbow on it. Well, I've always liked rainbows, so it was the first one I picked up. It would be the only flyer I looked at that day. I read the title, and then the first few lines.

It definitely grabbed my attention. It was titled *Always Our Children...* and the mission statement was printed on the cover. It read:

> The Body of Christ in the Diocese of Cleveland is called to reverence each person as a unique reflection of God's presence in our midst. We commit ourselves to become a community of care, support, formation, reconciliation and witness to justice with and among gay and lesbian persons, their parents, family members and all who minister in and with this community. We are here to help with any questions you may have. The Cleveland Diocesan patient/family support groups meet monthly.

Our meetings are open to all parents and family members. We hope that we will be help as you and your family make this journey. We know that these are challenging times for you and your child. Please know that we have been where you are now. For us too there was a time when we first learned that our son or daughter was gay. Through the gift of God's love and the help of others, our families, friends and Church, we have come to understand better our role as loving and supporting parents.

I continued to read the flier, enraptured by what was pulling at my subconscious. The pull was quickly becoming conscious, as I realized the text was describing something I desperately needed, but didn't know until now.

Love is the continuing story of every family's life. Love can be shared, nurtured, rejected and sometimes lost. To follow Christ's way of love is the challenge before every family today. Your family now has an added opportunity to share love and to accept love. Our church communities are likewise called to an exemplary standard of love and justice. Our homosexual sisters and brothers-indeed, all people are summoned into responsible ways of loving. Knowing that your child is Gay-How can you best express your love-itself a reflection of God's unconditional love for your child!

First, don't break off contact, don't reject your child! A shocking number of homosexual youth end up on the streets because of rejection by their families. This and other external pressures can place young people at greater risk of self-destructive behaviors, such as substance abuse and suicide. Your child may need you and the family now more than ever. He or she is still the same person. This child, who has always been God's gift to you, may now be the cause of another gift: your family becoming more honest, respectful and supportive.

Yes, your love can be tested by the reality, but it can also grow stronger than your struggle to respond loving-ly. Now is the time to be there for one another. Sexual Orientation is not something that is chosen. There seems to be no single cause of a homosexual orientation. A common opinion of experts is that there are multiple fac-tors-genetic, hormonal, and psychological-that may rise to it. Generally, homosexual orientation is experienced as a given, not as something freely chosen. All in all, it is essential to recall one basic truth. God loves every person as a unique individual. Sexual identity helps to define the unique persons we are and one component of our sexual identity is sexual orientation. Thus, our total personhood is more encompassing than sexual orientation. Human beings see the appearance, but the Lord looks into the heart of each of us. God does not love someone any less simply because he or she is homosexual. God's love is al-ways and everywhere offered to those who are open to receiving it.

I had no intention of joining a support group such as this. I never felt like I'd needed It. At the time I did not admit to anyone that I had gay chil-dren. I felt I was handling it the best I could and did not want to advertise information about my family to... *anyone*. I had no intention of coming out myself, or outing any of my children. After all, what if I attended a meeting and ran into someone I knew?

The more I began to think about these meetings the more curious I felt. I found myself looking at the clock on Sunday afternoons when I knew that the meeting was starting. I also felt as if I was losing a connection with my sons. I knew for certain that I wanted to be a good mom. No, not just a good mom, I wanted to be a MOM ... standing up for my children re-gardless of the consequences, no matter what the family dynamics were. The flyer made me realize it was past time for me to ask for help.

So, on a beautiful Sunday in April, I told my husband I was headed out to the store and knew I would not be missed. My husband was hooked on a baseball game and I could easily escape to my first meeting without suspicion. First, I rushed to the store to buy a couple of things to give my gimmick credibility. Then I arrived in the parking lot 30 minutes early and froze in the driver's seat as I watched people enter the building.

My confidence quickly evaporated. I was in a complete mental melt-down. My heart was racing and sweat beaded my forehead. I was so afraid to go inside. It wasn't a fear of talking in front of people. After all, as a community outreach nurse I had spoken to many audiences about bullying, drugs, alcohol, and the rest.

A few minutes before the meeting was to start I took a deep breath, opened my car door, and did not stop moving until inside. There were 18 people in attendance on that first day. They sat around tables pushed into a circle. The parish priest was there. That day the members consisted of parents of gays, lesbians, and bisexuals. Father "J" was very warm and soft-spoken. The meeting started with a quick prayer by Father and a gospel reading. There were a few couples, but most were moms like me who showed up solo.

I learned that the group was formed in 1999. Most in the group seemed to be in their 50s and 60s. The leaders were a bit older, maybe 70. They were a married couple with a lesbian daughter. They were warm and welcoming and focused on the purpose of our gathering, in full support of the mission. There seemed to be little to no trace of the guilt that weighed so heavily in my gut.

Deep inside, I still believed that I could have done something differently and my sons would not be gay. I was hoping that the support group would help me figure out what it was that I'd screwed up. I had tremendous guilt, and I worried often about being rejected by friends and family that might find out. My husband and I were new at parenting gay children and had no training or preparation for what was playing out for our children. Together we knew that somehow we needed to learn, grow and accept unconditionally the sexuality of our sons. That really wasn't the problem. The problem was would everyone else connected to us do the same.

Instead of finding the source of my guilt, to my surprise, the group was intent on helping me accept my sons... and myself.

There were several other nurses in the room, which eased my mind. The conversation started by going around the room to introduce ourselves. Father J asked us to mention a little tidbit about ourselves. They started with the folks that had been members for a while, but eventually it was my turn.

I was trembling, near tears and still in panic mode. All at once, I found words spilling from my mouth. I told them my name, my occupation, and the fact that I had 3 gay sons. You could hear the gasps (unless I imagined it) and then silence. I had tears in my eyes, trembled, and my voice was weak. As I glanced around the room I could not help but notice how they all looked directly at me with a caring and concerned look. They all knew how I was feeling inside.

Still, silence. The silence was oppressive.

"Yes," I repeated to them, "I have 5 amazing children and 3 of my sons are gay." I told them how I was living with the guilt that somehow I could have prevented it. I ended my 3-5 minute intro as tearless and tremble-free as I could. Just getting the words out took a weight off my chest. I hoped to lighten it up a bit so ended by saying, "I am certain that Oprah will be calling me any day for an interview to appear on her show." It worked.

Smiles erupted and the group assured me my feelings were both normal and manageable. I truly felt accepted for who I was and for the family that I represented. For the first time, I had admitted to others that I was the mom of gay children. This was the trial run of my personal "coming out" and the release was spiritual.

My secret trips to the support group continued. Each time I used the excuse to shop or run errands. Each time I would make sure I had a bag of something to take back in the house when I returned. I was not prepared to tell my spouse what I was really doing. I feared he would not understand. We did not have many conversations about our sons. It was tough for us to discuss. So I realized very quickly that the support group was my only outlet and my reinforcement that everything was going to be alright.

I learned so many things from the group's members. I thought early on that there would be no benefit from attending.

I.

Was.

Mistaken.

The information, friendship, and togetherness was an incentive to continue attending. Like Buck's, it was inspiration to write this book, too. It was the push I needed to communicate the truth that was growing stronger and stronger in my mind. We need to love and accept our children the way they have been given to us. What a novel, yet common sense, idea! How harsh our society is that it took me years to come to this conclusion.

I believe very strongly that the power of a community can bring out the support and equality that is needed. The conversations were always good, supportive, and eye opening. For example, many of the group expressed sadness that their LGBT adult children have left the church. You would think that because the church teaches love and compassion it would embrace these individuals.

Yet this is not the case. I realized the church does not honor LGBT openly. I am told that in the early development of this support group when the bishop of Cleveland asked three parishes to develop the LGBT support group, the start was so shaky it almost folded. None of the churches wanted to volunteer to hold these types of meetings. The bishop was forced to assign host churches instead since nobody volunteered to step forward.

There were three types of groups that attended first. The first was the Baptist group. They preached exodus for the LGBT. In other words, "pray for your children to leave homosexuality." The Baptist group felt that the devil inserted homosexuality in our children to test their faith and willpower. The Baptists were asked early on to cease their support group.

The second group was known as P-Flag. They were thrilled that Catholics were hosting the support group but kept pushing their agenda. Their agenda was to analyze the LGBT, presumably to find ways to "counter" the behaviors that many in the group believed was a choice. They prioritized this goal over providing support for families.

Finally, the third group wanted to support the cause and help with understanding and accepting LGBT youth.

For the sake of privacy and confidentiality, I will forgo the real names of my support group friends. I do feel that there were many conversations and shared information that are worth mentioning and valuable to the mission of this book. So with that, I would like to share the following redacted stories.

*   *   *   *   *

There was a long-time member of the group sitting across from me. I will call her Jean. She was a retired nurse in her 60s. Jean was fidgeting, anxious to share some bittersweet news. She had just returned from her daughter's out-of-town wedding in New York. Her daughter just married her female partner who has two children. Jean spoke of a beautiful ceremony with the little girls as flower girls. Jean admits she is thrilled to be a grandmother now. "I just love my two new granddaughters." But she went on to say that her three other children refused to attend the wedding. Their reason? Their sister married a woman.

Needless to say Jean was torn. She loved all of her children of course but, as any veteran parent knows, struggles over family cohesiveness are devastating. She has written a letter to the three siblings asking if they might've considered starting over as a family again.

None of the three children ever replied.

I think about her story often. What strikes me the most is the thought of Jean passing away someday and never seeing her family pull together again. I can't imagine leaving this world without my children loving and caring for each other. After my husband and I pass away, they'll be all that's left.

*   *   *   *   *

Another mom, let's call her Mary, once started a story by telling me that I look familiar. *Oh my goodness* is all I can think, *will this be good or bad? Do I make a loud noise to distract them and try to bolt from the room?* True to the group's supportive nature, she casually waved off my concerns with a bold familiarity.

Anyway, as she starts her story it turns out that her son knows my second son, Paul. She then opened up, expressing her fears for her gay son. Is his safety jeopardized because he is gay? Is he subject to abuse? Will he get HIV?

I have had these worries too, and for once I felt like I was in charge of soothing someone else's worries. And soothe I did. As her fears lessened, and the unknown slowly became known, her talk turned from worry to pride.

Mary proudly went on to tell the group that her son, J, invited her to dinner, one of twenty guests. She described it as formal and meticulous. She mentioned how proud and impressed she was. It was this dinner that she realized that her son had so many good qualities, was well-liked, and a very capable young man. "I couldn't be prouder," she said tearfully, "Gay or straight, he is a great kid!"

I knew what Mary was going through. The fear had subsided, and now all she wanted to do was brag about her awesome kids. She's right, our gay children are wonderful!

*   *   *   *   *

One woman, Chloe, once told us about her gay daughter who had recently announced her engagement to another woman. Chloe knew that she needed to react as she had when her son got engaged. She knew there'd be no excuse. Her daughter had already come out to her, so she'd be expected to already have processed her emotions.

Still, Chloe conceded that it was still difficult. "When my son got engaged to his girlfriend, I was thrilled and excited. I shouted the news to the world and smiled so much my face hurt! Yet my daughter announced her engagement to another woman and I almost shut down. I knew I had to act thrilled and excited. It took everything in me to express joy."

After she finished telling her troubles, I distinctly remember Chloe wiping tears from her eyes.

*   *   *   *   *

Another tells us that her son has dropped out of a local college in Ohio to move to Florida to stay with a man he hardly knew. She was worried and cried as she told us, "I know he is just trying to find himself."

This woman feared that he would take his life. She described her son as delicate and unsure of who he was, which made her worry about what he'd do about it.

We cried together as I gave her a hug. After all, I remembered my sons leaving home.

*   *   *   *   *

Jacob, a dad in the group, told us that he joined a well-known gay choir group in the area. He claimed that he was the only straight man in the entire group. His son was gay and Jacob was searching for any way to connect with him. He decided that joining the choir was an opportunity to show his son that he loved him.

As he told the story there wasn't a dry eye in the audience. "Plus," he chuckled, "I have a good singing voice."

After Jacob joined, his son began opening up to him. The refrain he heard from his son was similar to the one I heard at Buck's. Jacob's son told him that he felt a sense of unity in this [the choir] group. That he never felt hated or had to worry about being assaulted. With these men, he said, "I can relax and be me."

*   *   *   *   *

Here are some other great comments from the group I've heard over time:

"We do the best we can to love them. If we can't maintain a relationship with our gay child we have to hope and pray that a sincere someone will be there for them."

"We should always leave the door open and the light on for our child!"

One mom once told the group, "I don't want to tell anyone that my son is gay. My reason for this is if anyone hurts my son because of his sexuality or says something negative about my son I will make them regret it. If it were a friend or relative that did or said something negative about my son than that friendship or family relationship would come to an abrupt end."

Another mom responded, "Only those near and dear to my heart will know that my son is gay, because those are the ones that I would hope will understand and accept out of love."

A third said, "I won't tell anyone either. There are so many ignorant people in the world, and ignorance leads to hate."

"People will observe you and how you transmit your LGBT child. We must stand proud and supportive to show the world that our children matter!"

"Straight or gay they are our kids. No matter what, we love them." A father spoke those words. Hearing that from a father in the group was truly a powerful moment for all of us.

*   *   *   *   *

I hear many agree with each other that the holidays are tough. It is hard to tell family that your kids are gay. I understand that also. On occasion I have heard my father speak negatively about the gay community. It saddened me when he spoke his mind, but shame on me for not challenging him. Of course, these attitudes weren't held solely by my father.

A few years ago my husband and I attended a family Christmas gathering with our children. I overheard a relative make a negative comment about homosexuals. Another relative immediately tried to silence the comment and change the subject before it was overheard. I did overhear the comment, and it brought me close to tears. It was difficult for me to accept that this negative attitude had invaded our family's inner circle. It shocked me that someone who genuinely seemed to care about my family could be so hurtful and offensive. Yet, it was also a wakeup call—I learned that day how easily anti-LGBT sentiments were tossed around.

We have good days, bad days, and gay days. We are so proud of our kids so why can't we tell people about our kids being gay? Is opening up that tough? As the one woman said in our group, "We must stand proud and supportive! Our children matter"!

As we open up more we should become more comfortable talking about this. Some like to hate people who are different, to make themselves feel superior, and this is just another form of bullying, where adults are bullying adults.

My time in my support group was formative. I sat amongst so many wise parents in that room. Yet, even though we knew each other, everyone still struggled with letting their guard down. They couldn't breathe easy knowing that there are still people in this world that do not understand our children.

As I looked into the eyes and hearts of all those at the meetings, it opened my eyes to the harsh realities of life. We obviously love our LGBT children – "unconditionally, and we attend these meetings faithfully as a support and a tool to better understand our children and their sexuality.

Yet people like my father didn't do the same. They grew up in a time that lacked the vocabulary to talk about LGBT issues, so their experience lacked awareness of ideas about things like equality or non-discrimination.

Even in 2018 people can be obtuse. Most people don't experience the eye-popping education, emotional support, and inspirational love that pours forth. They don't experience the tears, or that it's okay to have gay children. They don't understand that LGBT is okay.

Sometimes I shudder to think what I'd be like if I didn't find that pamphlet.

What you learn in church is that faith comes gradually, and your faith is a gift. The same holds true with the trust of our children. Many LGBT individuals have left the church out of fear of rejection and discrimination. They shouldn't have to leave our homes, too.

Chemistry and relationships are so important to healing and mental well-being. I am convinced the best predictor for a successful life for a person is a loving relationship. We are all on the same river together. We are all from the same fabric and part of the same human family. We all have our own little bubbles that we live in and often we don't see outside of the bubble very well.

I wrote and delivered the following letter to the entire group on my last visit. I felt the need to stop attending so I could spend more time with my elderly father and make sure he had his traditional pasta dinner each Sunday. It read:

Dear Support Group Friends,

As I sit and write this I am very much aware of how much you have all become so important to me in a short period of time. I cannot attend our meeting today as I am visiting my son in Columbus for 3 days and then visiting my other son in Chicago for 4 days. Besides filling refrigerators, gas tanks and hanging a curtain or two, I am hoping to visit my favorite bars, "Bucks" and "Union" to reconnect with both my sons' friends I have grown very fond of.

Together we share in a very special journey of LOVE that no other group of parents will ever experience. I say this in a very positive way. We have been given a very special gift from God. We have been chosen to nurture and love very unique children. God knew what he was doing. He knew he could only give those children to parents that would embrace and love them so unconditionally. There was a time that I was once embarrassed, confused and ashamed of this unique circumstance. I have met such beautiful and loving people such as you, my son's friends, companions and others of the LGBT community. I am also blessed to think that God has chosen me to love three gay sons. He must have known that I could open and share my heart where others would not be capable of the same. I am complimented that he has selected my husband and I to be so right for this journey of love.

As you know, I am compelled to write a book. I want to tell the story, share our feelings and thoughts with the world. It is through our eyes and our children's eyes that we will help the world gain love, respect and peace towards our children and their sexuality. I have one goal in writing this book and that is to open the hearts and minds of those who do not fully understand our journey. As I said in my opening sentence

*of this letter, you are very special to me. I would <u>never, ever</u>
violate your privacy or share information that would offend
you. I would not use your names or tell a story that would lead
to identifying your family and loved ones. Please understand
that this will be a slow, well thought out process and will move
very cautiously through its development stages. A message
and mission such as ours must be delicately and carefully
constructed to meet such important goals. I want this book
to illustrate a sincere picture of our mission and love for our
children. I want to focus on your analogies and quotes of wisdom. This book is intended to be a guideline and turning point
for all who read it to see the truth and the light of this special
journey.*

    *Thank you for all you have done to make me a better parent,
which is my most important role in life.*

                      Sincerely,
                      Paula

**   *   *   *   **

Several years ago my husband and I joined four other couples hosting
the Pre-Cana Day at our church. Pre-Cana Day is a Catholic requirement
for engaged couples to attend prior to their wedding. Our duties varied
somewhat, but the focus is to enhance relationships by sharing information with them. We hoped to help them dig deep into their feelings of love
and commitment and faith.

Our mission is to prepare them for a solid and loving marital relationship. We cover several topics throughout the day, mostly advice on how to
cultivate a successful marriage with things like communication, compromise, faith, and commitment. Although I do not claim to be an expert with
any of these topics, I am a firm believer that these areas are the very fiber
that keeps any relationship solid and connected. It may sound selfish, but
I look forward to this day as a confirmation and renewal of my own marital
relationship with my husband. We have experienced marital challenges
and strains at times. Thus any moment or small gesture that we can share
to confirm our commitment is important and vital in my eyes.

As I stated earlier in this book, I often thought I may have been the
blame for my children's sexuality. I often wondered if my husband felt

that way as well. I have no explanation for why I felt this way but for several years we had many more questions than we did educated answers.

Knowing that 3 of our 4 sons are gay led us to experience the grief of lost expectations. Sadness and concern for all they have had to endure on their own, but so grateful for their inner strength and courage. We did the only thing we thought we should do – shower them with unconditional love. We made it a priority to focus on our children at all times knowing that this is all part of the Plan for us. It was our normal.

Relationships come in many looks and styles. The look and style doesn't matter. What matters is a solid foundation. Love, respect, and happiness are the byproducts of a solid relationship. A strong relationship needs to complement and enhance each person in the relationship. A good relationship brings out the best in both people. Each person makes the other person a better human being. These are the formula to a relationship, not race, age, or sexuality. Base it on truth, love and commitment to maintain that solid relationship.

You have to teach others how you want to be treated. Finding your perfect relationship is like finding a treasure. To find your treasure you must be on a treasure hunt (unfortunately there's never a map!). If you are without someone to love you, to motivate you, and support you, you may never believe in yourself or accomplish your life goals. Marriage is about people who love each other.

Longtime LGBT couples perceive their relationships as being just as committed to each other as married heterosexuals do. Honestly, it's an insult to the LGBT to assume otherwise. Assuming otherwise assumes that they are somehow lesser.

Until the Supreme Court decision in 2015, many LGBT couples held commitment ceremonies to celebrate their relationship formally, in the company of friends and family. More LGBT couples are becoming partners and spouses than ever. Some lesbians are using artificial inseminations to conceive a child they can raise with their partner. Other LGBTs who came out after they have been involved in heterosexual relationships are raising children from those marriages with their partners. Also more and more LGBT couples are adopting.

The lesson is: When someone makes you truly happy, magnifies the good in you and makes you feel like you are everything you have always wanted to be, then what else matters? The answer to that question, of course, is nothing.

CHAPTER 6

LGBT Politics

Let's get the most important point out of the way: homosexuality is not a mental disorder.

In 1973 the American Psychiatric Association removed homosexuality from the Diagnostic Manual.[11] This signified the end to its official classification as a disease.

Some psychologists classify every emotion as either love (attraction) or fear (aversion). It is not unusual for humans to base almost every decision on fear. Fear drives many of our base impulses as humans. Fear of rejection, fear of looking stupid, etc... You should recognize discrimination between fear-based and love-based decisions. Love-based decisions come for our inner essence, not from external pressures or anxieties. We will still have energy and strength after a love-based decision is made.

Imagine the decisions we would make if we had no fear of failing, losing, or being alone. Every choice or decision is either going to enhance or drain your spirit. Don't betray what is in your heart. When your life begins to harm you and falsify who you are, know that you have taken a detour from your true path.

Consulting a therapist in the hopes of changing your child's sexual orientation is pointless. Homosexuality is not a disease to be cured. Homosexuality is a natural way of being. Because homosexuality is not chosen you cannot change your child's mind. The American Psychological Association and the American Medical Association have taken the official position that it would be unethical to even try to change the sexual orientation of a gay person. In 1997, the American Psychological Association publicly cautioned against so called "conversion therapy" and in 2010 the APA released a statement warning against the mischaracterizations of legislative efforts dealing with homosexuality.[12]

It is, however, a good idea to consult a therapist if your child is having difficulties dealing with their situation. A mental health professional can help them navigate their troubles. You may want to talk to someone about your own feelings and how to work through them. You might feel that you and your child need help communicating clearly through this period. You may recognize that your child is unhappy and needs help with self-acceptance. This too would warrant consultation.

Gay people often have trouble accepting themselves and their sexual identity. In this circumstance, self-rejection could be a dangerous emotional state. There are a number of options and resources. A therapist can also provide the confidentiality and anonymity that you may feel you need. There are a variety of resources for help, information and advice. I encourage you to explore your options that would best suit your family's needs. Unfortunately, until more organizations become advocates for LGBT rights, your child does face some significant challenges.

Right brain oriented people are those where the dominant hemisphere is the one controlling intuition. They are more likely to be more creative than those with left brain orientation. Right brain people are creative and artistic, they are more coincidence-conscious and the left-brained tend toward logic and mathematical skills. The left brain is also more concerned with numbers, reasoning and reading, etc.

The bottom line is not everyone is the same, and you shouldn't expect others to be like you... or your kids. Don't follow the crowd, be yourself, believe in something, and reach beyond your bubble.

*   *   *   *   *

Governor Gregoire introduced historic legislation that would allow same-sex marriages in Washington State in 2012.[13] While fighting for legislation she commented, "Our gay and lesbian families face the same hurdles as heterosexual families — making ends meet, choosing what school to send their kids to, finding someone to grow old with, standing in front of friends and family and making a lifetime commitment." [13]

In the 2015 Supreme Court case *Obergefell v. Hodges*, the court ruled that the denial of marriage licenses to same-sex couples and the refusal to recognize those marriages performed in other jurisdictions violates the Due Process and the Equal Protection clauses of the Fourteenth Amendment of the United States Constitution.[14] The ruling overturned a 1972 precedent, *Baker v. Nelson*.[15] Just prior to the Supreme Court's ruling in

2015, same-sex marriage was legal in many, but not all U.S. jurisdictions, thanks to grassroots efforts that led to state-wide legislation.

While civil rights campaigning took place primarily in the 1970s, the issue of same-sex marriage became prominent in 1993 when the Hawaiian Supreme Court ruled in *Baehr v. Lewin* that the prohibition was unconstitutional.[15, 16] The ruling led to federal actions and initiatives led by several states to restrict marriage to male-female couples, in particular the *Defense of Marriage Act* (DOMA).[17] During the period of 2003 to 2015, various lower court decisions, state legislation, and popular referendums already legalized same-sex marriage to some degree in thirty-eight out of fifty U.S. states, in the U.S. territory of Guam, and in the District of Columbia.

Then, in 2013, the Supreme Court overturned a key provision of DOMA, with Justice Kennedy declaring part of it unconstitutional and in breach of the Fifth Amendment in *United States v. Windsor* because it singled out a class of persons for discrimination, by refusing to treat their marriages equally under federal law when state law had created them equally valid.[17] This ruling essentially started a domino effect that led to the federal government's recognition of same-sex marriage, with federal benefits for married couples connected to either the state of residence or the state in which the marriage was solemnized. However, the ruling was rather limited in nature, focusing entirely on the provision of DOMA responsible for the federal government refusing to acknowledge state sanctioned same-sex marriages, leaving the question of state marriage laws itself to the individual states. The Supreme Court would later address that question two years later in 2015, ruling in *Obergefell* that same-sex married couples were to be constitutionally accorded the same recognition as opposite-sex couples at state/territory levels, as well as at federal level.

By the time that same-sex marriage became legal nationally, public opinion on the subject reached approval levels of 57%, while the number opposed was a mere 35%.[18] This is notable because these were approval ratings in 2001. Since then, support has grown steadily while holdouts around the nation gradually concede that homosexuality is an unavoidable genetic truth, and not harming them in any way. Today, 62% of Americans approve of gay marriage.[18]

* * * * *

Our LGBT are actively serving in the military as well. As of May 2010, an estimated 48,500 LGBT were serving in the armed forces in either active duty or ready reserve.[19] This accounts for 2.2% of all military personnel. Women make special mention, too. Despite representing less than 15% of all active duty members, women composed more than 40% of LGBT members.[19]

*   *   *   *   *

Until a few years ago, sexual orientation was referred to as sexual preference. Obviously the two terms denote significant differences in the manner by which sexuality develops. A preference is something that is chosen, whereas orientation is something that defines us. The differences are extremely important to understand human sexuality.

Male and female fetuses are often exposed to similar amounts of testosterone. Levels of the hormone can be even higher than normal in females and lower in males without any effect on genital or brain structure. Gene structure is not affected by the hormone changes but effect how the gene is chemically altered or activated. It was also determined that homosexuality may be a carry-over from one's parent's own prenatal resistance to the hormones of the opposite sex. As I stated earlier in the book, 10% of the world population is LGBT, and homosexuality tends to run in families. Remember, 40% of those in homeless shelters are LGBT and were ostracized by none other than their own parents.

Regarding how the law applies to those who are gay, if homosexuality is not chosen, but actually is a biologically-determined characteristic over which we have no choice, then laws should not treat gays and straights differently. Thus homosexuality would be equivalent to one's race over which we have no control. Sexual expression, whether it be heterosexual, homosexual, or bisexual is an orientation not a behavior, not a preference, nor is it an addiction or a lust. Sexual orientation defines the emotional, romantic, and sexual attraction a person has for the opposite sex, same sex or both sexes. We can each choose what we do with our sexual desires, but we cannot change sexual orientation.

CHAPTER 7

LGBT Research

THE LGBT COMMUNITY SUFFERS DUE TO SOCIETY'S ATTITUDES

Headed by researcher Caitlin Ryan, her Family Acceptance Project looked at the effects of family acceptance and rejection on physical and mental health, and the well-being of LGBT youth. It was the first study of its kind.[20]

The study looked at factors including rates of suicide, HIV, and homelessness. Their research shows that LGBT youths who experienced high levels of rejection from their families during adolescence, compared to those that received little or no rejection, were 8 times more likely to attempt suicide, 6 times more likely to suffer high levels of depression, and 3 times more likely to be at high risk for HIV, STD, drug or alcohol addiction.[20]

Numerous studies have shown that LGBT youth have a higher rate of suicide attempts than do heterosexual youths. The CDC estimates that nearly 40% of LGBT youths have attempted suicide.[21] This higher prevalence of suicidal ideation and overall mental health problems among LGBT teens compared to heterosexual teens has been attributed to stress and negative acceptance from others, specifically parents and their families. Suicide is the 3rd leading cause of death among 15-24 year olds.[21]

The conclusions reached by the Family Acceptance Project is backed by nearly every clinical trial, psychological experiment, or sociological investigation devoted to the plights of the LGBT community. One of my favorite and comprehensive resources surrounding this topic is the book *Stigma and Sexual Orientation: Understanding Prejudice Against Lesbians, Gay Men, and Bisexuals*. In it, editor Gregory M. Herek compiled a massive collection of research that investigates minority stress, societal forces that shape attitudes toward the LGBT, and proved through a large con-stellation of studies and statistical data that the LGBT community suffers higher rates of violence, health problems, and social stigmatization.[22]

Herek's research looks beyond the surface to scratch at a myriad of top-ics to back up his claims. In one chapter, he proves that juries are more likely to convict members of the LGBT community due to homophobic bi-ases.[22] In another, he analyzes how social forces make it difficult for LGBT couples to engage in deep levels of intimacy because of the psychological damage that is involved with a lifetime of struggle. He also investigates developmental problems, civil rights issues around the globe, victimiza-tion, LGBT parenting, and voter attitudes associated with the LGBT com-munity. Herek's work is disheartening but recommended reading for any-one who believes that the main issue surrounding the LGBT community is simply about gay marriage. It's about so much more.[22]

HOMOSEXUALITY IS DEFINITELY DUE, IN PART, TO GENETICS

Evolutionary geneticist, William Rice of the University of California has conducted studies to determine if homosexuality is the result of gene variations in the womb.[4] Sexual development occurs both neurologically and morphologically. Morphological development, in the absence of any hormonal influence, genetically male or female fetuses will develop morphologically as female.[24] Male sexual development requires testosterone, estrogen and dihydrotestosterone. Female sexual development can occur in either the presence or absence of estrogen. The sex hormones that operate during development are produced by either the testes or ovaries and the adrenal glands. In regard to neurological development, sexual orientation is associated with the establishment of permanent differences in the hypothalamic and limbic areas of the brain. Sex-typical behavior patterns are associated with changes in diverse areas of the brain and extensively involving the cortex.[24]

In 2012, a group of scientists suggested that homosexuals get their trait from their opposite sex parents.[25] A lesbian will almost always get the trait from her father, while a gay man will get the trait from his mother. Though scientists have long suspected some sort of genetic link why people are gay, the explanations have been few and far between. Most mainstream biologists have shied away from studying why people are gay because of the social stigma. In other words, people are still stuck on the idea that homosexuality is unnatural, despite homosexuality appearing naturally in people.

Research shows it appears natural in animals as well. Homosexual behavior has been observed in a whopping 1,500 different animal species, including dolphins, some types of whales, apes, crabs, worms, giraffes, several different types of birds, and penguins.[26]

*   *   *   *   *

A simple way of looking at the complexities of human sexuality is the Kinsey Scale.[27] It classifies exclusively opposite-sex attracted individuals to strongly same-sex attracted individuals on a scale ranging 0-6. The Kinsey Scale is an idea developed by Alfred Kinsey in 1948 that instead of describing people as either homosexual, heterosexual, or bisexual, sexual orientation was really a scale from heterosexuality to homosexuality. Figure 1 on the following page exhibits this scale and its meaning.[27]

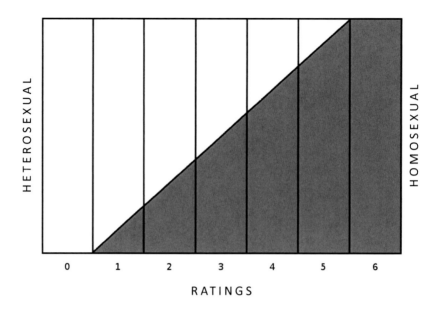

Figure 1. The Kinsey Scale, a visual graph demonstrating sexuality along a gradient

Rating | *Description*
0 | *Exclusively heterosexual*
1 | *Predominantly heterosexual, only incidentally homosexual*
2 | *Predominantly heterosexual, but more than incidentally homosexual*
3 | *Equally heterosexual and homosexual*
4 | *Predominantly homosexual, but more than incidentally heterosexual*
5 | *Predominantly homosexual, only incidentally heterosexual*
6 | *Exclusively homosexual*
X | *No socio-sexual contacts or reactions*

The Kinsey team interviewed thousands of people about their sexual histories. Research showed that sexual behavior, thoughts, and feelings towards the same or opposite sex were not always consistent across time.[27] Instead of assigning people to three categories—heterosexual, bisexual, and homosexual—the team used a seven-point scale. It ranges from 0 to 6 with an additional category of "X." [27]

Kinsey Scale tests, later developed on the ideas introduced by Kinsey, seem to have good predictive power. [28]

KINSEY SCALE TEST

What is your age? _____
What gender do you identify as? ❒ Man ❒ Woman

Please evaluate the following statements as either true or false were you to say them.

I have never felt sexual desire.
 ❒ True ❒ False

I can not decide what sex I am attracted to more.
 ❒ True ❒ False

I find the idea of having sex with another ["man" if male, "woman" if female] repulsive.
 ❒ True ❒ False

I wouldn't want to die without having experimented sexually with both men and women.
 ❒ True ❒ False

I have no interest in sexual intercourse with anyone.
 ❒ True ❒ False

The gender composition of an orgy would be irrelevant to my decision to participate.
 ❒ True ❒ False

I avoid watching ["gay" if male, "lesbian" if female] pornography.
 ❒ True ❒ False

I can be sexually attracted to anyone in the right circumstances.
 ❒ True ❒ False

I have always been extremely confident in my sexual orientation.
 ❒ True ❒ False

I find ["men" if male, "women" if female] more attractive than ["women" if male, "men" if female].
 ❒ True ❒ False

I would find a threesome with a couple awkward specifically because of the presence of the ["man" if male, "woman" if female].
 ❒ True ❒ False

I am only attracted to ["women" if female, "men" if male].
 ❒ True ❒ False

I am sexually submissive.
 ❒ True ❒ False

Chapter 8

The LGBT Parent/Child Survey

At the very early stages of planning this book, I knew through my research, my visits to Columbus and Chicago, and my connections with the LGBT community that I needed to conduct a survey to be included in this publication. The first day that the survey was distributed to many of the LGBT community, I received an outpouring of response. It amazed me how many people were anxious to share their feelings and their stories. They were hungry to come out – to have a book to assist them, to support them, and to help them claim their identity.

To follow are sample survey questions and stats/graphs that identify the responses and conclusions of this project.

The Survey As It Was Presented:

I am writing a book called "Always Our Children." The purpose of this book is to educate and support parents and families of LGBT children. This book is intended to open the eyes of families and friends of LGBT children. I am hoping to assist families to fully understand the life and feelings that LGBT children experience.

You do not need to give your name with this survey unless you would like to. This survey will remain confidential and only used to gather data that will be suitable to enhance the goals of this book. Thank you in advance for your contribution to the educational experience of this topic.

SURVEYS DISTRIBUTED: 75
RESPONSES: 63

What is your date of birth?

AGE OF RESPONDERS
22   41

What is your gender?

MALE RESPONDERS   49

FEMALE RESPONDERS   14

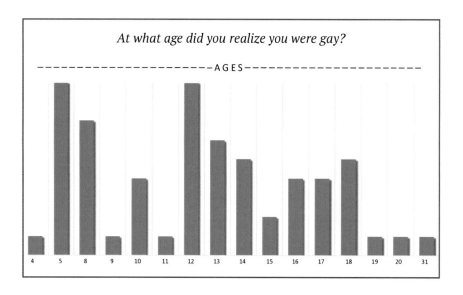

At what age did you realize you were gay?

————————————————AGES————————————————

4   5   8   9   10   11   12   13   14   15   16   17   18   19   20   31

Was it clear to you at the time that you were gay?

What was the time frame you needed to figure this out?

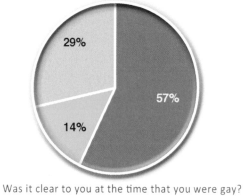

29%

57%

14%

Was it clear to you at the time that you were gay?

█ YES   █ NO   █ Somewhat

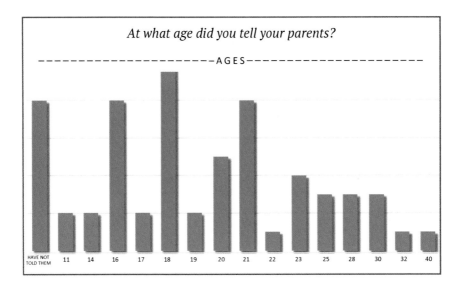

At what age did you tell your parents?

- A G E S -

HAVE NOT TOLD THEM   11   14   16   17   18   19   20   21   22   23   25   28   30   32   40

How did you tell them?
How did they react?

WRITE-IN COMMENTS WORTH MENTIONING:

- My mother did not talk to me for 2 weeks she looked at me as if I was a creature
- My parents told me they were very disappointed in me
- My mom threatened to kill my companion at the time
- My dad told me he would arrange therapy for me
- My dad said, "How can we fix this?"
- My mother cried and walked away
- They said they already knew and were supportive
- My mother was sad because she wanted me to have children
- My dad said "you are not gay and don't tell your mother"
- My dad said, "How could you do this to our family?"
- They kicked me out, I have no connection with them to this day
- Very accepting
- My mother said, "okay, but do not bring a man to this house"
- They were angry and made very ignorant comments
- My mom told me that I should get help, I moved out
- My mom said, you are my son and I love you, let's not tell your father
- My mother sobbed
- Hesitant but accepting a short time later
- They told me I was just going through a phase
- They wished me happiness in "my decision".
- My dad said, "I feel sorry for your future"
- They said they "always knew"
- My dad said, "you know you can't live here anymore"
- My mom sad because she worried for my safety she said.
- I went back into the closet since my parents were so upset.
- I am 35 years old and my parents still do not accept that I am gay
- They disowned me and sent me to Military School
- My Mom was great, My dad called me a confused teen, he still does not accept me
- I hope my parents read your book, Paula. I hope they will learn to accept me.
- Thank you for writing this book, parents need help understanding us better

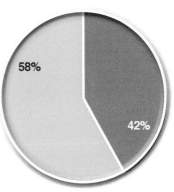

58%

42%

What was your parent's reaction?

 POSITIVE   NEGATIVE

I feel accepted at work. Explain.

I have been a victim of bullying. Explain.

My best friend is gay.

I have had thoughts of hurting myself or suicide. Explain.

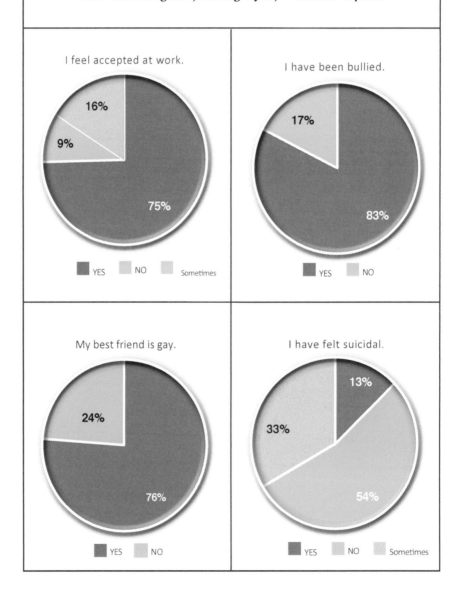

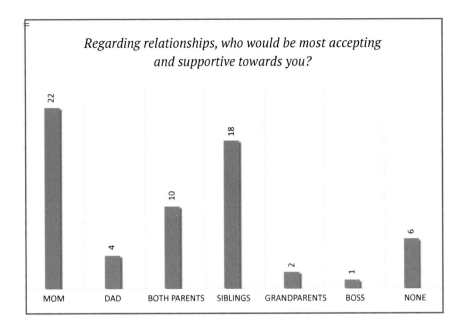

Regarding relationships, who would be most accepting and supportive towards you?

MOM	DAD	BOTH PARENTS	SIBLINGS	GRANDPARENTS	BOSS	NONE
22	4	10	18	2	1	6

OTHER QUESTIONS INCLUDED ON THE ORIGINAL SURVEY:

My best friend is ❏ male   ❏ female

I am accepted by my family. Explain

I feel safe where I live. Explain

Which family member communicates with you easily about your sexuality?

What would you like everyone to know about you and your sexuality?

Who is the most supportive person in your life? Describe this person and why you feel this way.

Give advice as to what one should do when "coming out".

List 5 things that have been a positive impact in regard to your sexuality:

List 5 things that have been a negative impact in regard to your sexuality:

The one thing I would change that would improve my self-esteem & pride is:

My parents would make my life much easier if:

What is the biggest challenge (present day) when considering my sexuality?

How does this differ from 10 years ago?

Please feel free to add any comments or suggestions here:

CHAPTER 9

Modern Day

Before I get into the modern day news cycle, I'd like to state my opinions on what it means to be LGBT in today's society – and in today's church.

It is very clear that our society's notion of what the word "family" means has changed and will continue to evolve over time. There may no longer be such a thing as a typical or traditional family. Though our concept of family may have changed, what hasn't changed is that family life is challenging. This is partially due to diversity. Diversity should be celebrated and owned by a family, not used to define battle lines between its members.

Being part of a family, be it blended, single parent, multicultural, adoptive, multi-generational, mixed faith or traditional requires that we embrace the ability to accompany each other. Accompanying someone means to walk with them through whatever situation they are experiencing. It means to be there for them, to support them, and listen without necessarily trying to change or fix their situation.

The truth is we can only define ourselves. The only person we can change is ourself, and attempting to change others goes against the very individualism that we celebrate as Americans. We can offer love, support, and encouragement when asked, but each person must act to change themselves. The best that we can do is to be with the members of our family and accept them for who they are. Accompanying family members means allowing them to learn to deal with difficult circumstances or to make mistakes and learn from them. It means allowing them to live their own lives and make their own choices. Accompanying is about a connection, a connection between people which flows from love and respect and which leads to support and acceptance. Accompanying is how Mary and Joseph treated Jesus. Joseph and Mary didn't completely understand what

Jesus was called to do nor could they do it for him, so they walked with him. Our lives are influenced by how we interact with the members of our family. By accompanying one another through challenges and difficulties of life, we grow closer to and connect more deeply with those in our family.

The church has said homosexuality is a sin. Or worse yet, a sinful choice. Are LGBT really offending God for the way that God made *them?* The answer, of course, is no. God accepts everyone. My sons are not sinners. Everyone should have the opportunity to find love. The sin would be assuming that they should not be able to freely love without fear and guilt. The sin would be not allowing them to accept themselves.

Some find it challenging to question God and instead many individuals simply conclude that God surpasses all understanding (Philippians 4:7). This idea implies that there is no way to discover the reasoning of God's plan and that it should simply be accepted during times of adversity. Many of the Psalms deal with someone who needed God to comfort them in times of struggle. What about King David? Abraham? Moses leading his people through the desert? These were men who followed God, yet they still asked questions to divine meaning and inspire their own actions.

Humans are destined to endure struggle, regardless of who you are, where you live, or in what time period. Although individuals may be destined to endure struggle throughout life, it does not mean that these struggles should rule over them. It is hard to imagine that a loving God creates violence and suffering to bait humans into mistakes. Perhaps God stands as a bystander of the world waiting to give people hope through times of adversity. Could it be that God does not cause the bad things that happen to us? Rather, he stands ready to help us cope with our tragedies – if we could only get beyond the feelings of guilt and anger that separate us from him.

It is possible that God observes the struggle in the world so people find refuge in him. After seeing such negativity in the world, maybe God is merely waiting for humans to find hope in him. Since it is so easy to see the destruction, corruption, and struggle in today's world, some may find it comforting to remain faithful to a loving and caring God.

Personally, I find it hard to imagine that God does not have control over a world that he created. Saint Augustine questioned the wisdom of God and how his wisdom affected the world. He stated, "God would not allow any evil to exist unless out of it he could draw a greater good."[29]

Augustine's belief was that free will wasn't rooted in the things we cannot control, but the things we can. The Bible has plenty to say about free will, too. The Book of Proverbs describes free will, proclaiming "The heart of man plans his way, but the Lord establishes in his steps through commandments" (Matthew 19:17). The Gospel of Mark tells us that there is nothing greater than to "Love your neighbor as yourself." Furthermore, "greater love has no one than this: to lay down one's life for one's friends" (John 15:13).

Putting others before ourselves and supporting them is the highest import of God's reasoning. And love. Maybe God isn't all powerful, but He is still always ready to help. In the end, the only thing we can really do is love one another through our struggles, praise God for the good He has done for our world, and maintain hope in His everlasting kingdom.

I recently heard a reading at church that speaks well of forgiveness, compassion, and the point of love:

> Clothe yourselves then as lifting for god's chosen people, holy and beloved of him. Put on compassion, kindness, humility, meekness, and patience to bear with one another and forgive whenever there is any occasion to do so. As the Lord has forgiven you, forgive one another. Above all, clothe yourselves with love which binds everything together in perfect harmony. May the peace of Christ overflow in your hearts, for this end you were called to be one body. And be thankful.
>
> - Colossians 3:12-17

We must realize that God awaits somewhere else as we move toward the light that is God. Faith gets a bad rap because the attitudes within that fear change. There are so many people of faith that are supportive. I was given three gay sons as a gift from God. The Catholic Church teaches that above everything else we have primacy of conscience. But how does this primacy do us any good if we use it to persecute others for factors beyond their control?

Standing up for what you believe in is not always easy. But that is how change happens. That is what I'm doing. And by publishing this book, and going against members of my own institution, I'm following in the steps of Jesus.

Jesus paid a terrible price for standing up for what he believed in. He paid with death. We parents must move from our initial tears and fears into the fire of advocacy. Parents can and do add an extra dimension to the Catholic LGBT equal justice movement. We must leave room for God to walk through the room. Is there a future for gay and lesbian Catholics? They need and hope for greater acceptance and greater emphasis on love. Marriage is one of the largest front lines in America's secular culture wars. Church vs LGBT is a struggle between the bishops and the LGBT Catholics over LGBT marriage. This is the most prominent issue facing LGBT today, because huge portions of the country are religious, and being LGBT doesn't recognize cultural boundaries. LGBT persons exist in every facet of society.

The common ground between LGBT Catholics and the church is their agreement that respecting human dignity, compassion and sensitivity must be emphasized at all times. The damage that can be done to people because they feel unaccepted, uncomfortable, and hated by the church can be horrific. It is sad to me that people walk away or feel driven away from the church because of their sexuality. I love going to church. I love being inside my church. It is a beautiful church. Inside, I feel comfortable. Somehow, when I am at a low point, going to church lifts me up. Attending church and praying can be very therapeutic. Yet people like me all over the country have gay and lesbian offsprings who are terrified by the very warmth that I enjoy. And it's all because they don't feel accepted.

I do believe He hears us. I admit that there are times that I do not always absorb and understand the message of the Sunday gospel or our readings. But somehow, simply being present and a part of the mass celebration fulfills my feeling of faith and purpose. Just last week, I did understand the message and it was one I appreciated. Our priest said, among other things, "We are people of truth, love, hope and goodness. We should always live a life of truth and goodness." There it is! He said it all. Spoken by our parish priest himself. These words convince me that our LGBT children should be accepted with open arms.

Those with no personal extensive experiences with the gay community seem to let their biases support their prejudices, which continues to poison our churches and conservative communities with half-truths.

We raised our children Catholic. Thus, today, I interviewed one of my gay sons on his thoughts about religion. He had much to say. Here is a portion of what he said:

> "God doesn't punish people. Only people punish people and themselves. Loves is love and it comes in many shapes, sizes etc... Religion needs to adapt to the constantly changing environment, society, people, etc..."

The one thing that church cannot afford to do is refuse to pay attention to what is actually happening in people's lives. Perhaps they need to look at the ongoing changes of marital unions. It may be God showing us, the church, the need to recognize and respond to God's own work in nontraditional marriages. Catholic leaders are supposed to tend to the flock, but by ignoring the LGBT community they are allowing part of the flock to be devoured by wolves. I had hoped for better acceptance and greater focus on love from my spiritual leaders.

God is trying to tell us that through our evolving world and rapidly-changing society we must all adapt with compassion. Being Catholic is a heart issue. Being nourished spiritually is how Catholics need to live in their faith. In time the church will change, as did slavery, women's rights, etc... and the Holy Spirit will shake things up because the Holy Spirit is in charge!"

I was glad I asked my son. I liked his analysis and he is wise beyond his years.

The *Always Our Children* support group gives the truest, clearest message to LGBT Catholics. Whenever I reflect on these words, I feel once again at home within my faith. When asked, they offered a statement:

The Bishop wrote, "In you, God is revealed. There is no fear in love. Perfect love drives away fear. Go out into the world and make disciples of people in every nation." The call only speaks to every man and woman of good will, every culture, every being under God's watch. He is mindful of the abiding dignity of every human person. The Catholic Bishops reaffirm that LGBT people like everyone else should not suffer from prejudice against their basic human rights. They have a right to respect, right to friendship and to justice. They should have an active role in the Christian Community. Jesus told his disciples in his sermon on the mount, saying, "Blessed are the meek for they shall inherit the Earth. Blessed are those that have truly accepted who they are, who are true to themselves, for they will inherit the world. I am life," Jesus continued, "and you are the truth and the light of life."

For some parents, this may be the most difficult issue to face.

It's a non-issue. It is true that some religions continue to condemn homosexuality. But even within these religions, there are respected leaders who believe that their church's position of condemnation is unconscionable. In 1997, the US Catholic Bishops issued a pastoral statement urging parents to love and support their gay children. In a 1994 pastoral letter, the US Episcopal bishops wrote, "As it can be for heterosexual persons, the experience of steadfast love can be for homosexual persons an experience of God."

Many mainstream American religions now have taken official stands in support of LGBT rights. Some have gone further. The Methodist Church, for example, has developed a network of reconciling congregations welcoming LGBT persons. Since 1991, The United Church of Christ has had a denominational policy stating that sexual orientation should not be a barrier to ordination. In the Episcopal Church, the denomination's legislative body has declared LGBT people have a full and equal claim with all other people upon the church. You will still hear people quote the Bible in defense of their prejudice against gay people. But many Biblical scholars dispute any anti gay interpretations of Biblical texts.

Have you ever been in a completely dark room? It's hard to see or know where anything is. But think of the effect when a light source suddenly shines. Just a bit of light and so much becomes visible. That is how powerful light can be. Light is such a common theme in scripture and liturgy that we might overlook or miss the strength of that message. So, slow down and ask what this means when viewing our gay children.

Light gives insight. Turn on the light and see what is really there. The light can help you see what is at the root of the way you are feeling. Not only can you see what hurts and makes you unsure of things, but the light should also draw your eye to the love you have for your child. Perhaps that love has been hidden. This could easily change how you look at your child and how to move forward in love.

Light gives us perspective. Darkness keeps us from understanding the big picture. It is easy to focus narrowly on how having a gay child affects us personally. However, it is best to take a panoramic view of our children and try to check out the entire plan God has for our life. Your loving relationship will illuminate once your light leads you to mutual respect, trust, and love with your child. Instead of focusing on disappointment, you need to focus on the blessing.

Light also gives us hope. In the dark, we fear what we can't see. But light shows us where we are going. If you are uncertain with your feelings,

God's light can bring hope. He may not show you exactly what to do, but he will remind you where we are going. His light can draw your vision to the destination and goal. So, love your children with all your heart and let that love be your light.

*   *   *   *   *

In a single week, three different gay men were attacked in Columbus. All three attacks were independent of one another. These attacks weren't nothing. One man was beaten so severely walking home, the orbital bone in his face was fractured. Another was beaten with a club and robbed less than five blocks from his home while he was out for a walk. The third was assaulted outside a gay bar, and he left with a concussion and a fractured jaw.

Despite the terrible frequency by which this happens all around the country, what happened next was absolutely amazing. Columbus LGBT allies in the community started a movement in pink. Pink t-shirts were distributed to the community by the thousands and worn to support the gay community.

The Buckeye Region Anti-Violence Organization (BRAVO) keeps track of violence against people in Ohio because of sexual orientation. One of their spokesmen, Andrew Leavitt described the situation saying, "When people are attacked because of who they are something needs to be done. You can really be altered for the rest of your life. We need to find a way to cope with this and feel safe in our environment that we call home."

Leavitt posted on Facebook, calling his supporters to wear pink on Friday. Countless local businesses went pink as well, selling pink food, pink t-shirts, pink ice cream, and so much more. Over $11,000 was raised on "Pink Friday" and a website was developed creating positive awareness for the community. The attacks, and the response to the attacks, revitalized the community and woke them up to the truth about today: just because it's 2018 doesn't mean the most diverse among our society are any safer. The beauty of this movement was that not only did they take a negative event and turn it into a positive, but because it developed organically and genuinely.

There is hope! Many cities and communities across our country are working to decriminalize homosexual behavior and recognize homosexuality as natural. These jurisdictions have taken measures to ensure non-discrimination. While enforcement is usually rare among individuals, anti-gay laws are often used against LGBT. Many states have repealed disputes, legal actions, and attempts to discriminate against individuals on the basis of sexual orientation. I think it's noteworthy that the LGBT segregated themselves for safety and cohesiveness, because it shows how little they are able to trust us, the mainstream.

Last year, Cleveland State University opened a new LGBT center on its campus, and someone anonymously posted a flyer on campus urging gay students to kill themselves.[30] The University reacted immediately, but the door had been flung open and outside commentators showed just how resiliently a society can protect its harshest biases. The policy director at the American Civil Liberties Union, Mike Brickner, stated that criminalizing these types of communal distractions should be protected, lest we as a society trample over free speech rights.[30] And unfortunately, there is a bit of truth to that. That's why it's so important that we, as a society, change the way we think about innate, unchangeable, personality traits.

Sometimes you simply can't reverse a lifetime of bigoted thinking. And for that we have the criminal justice system. That's why last year California passed the LGBT Senior Bill of Rights which was enacted to protect LGBTs from the harshest, most bigoted or fundamentalist groups attempting to deny the LGBT community its rights.[31] The law effectively helps LGBT seniors in nursing homes and hospice care. It also penalizes people for refusing to use an LGBTs respective pronoun.[31]

Sen. Scott Weiner, the bill's author, released a statement the day the bill went into law:

> "Our LGBT seniors built the modern LGBT Community and led the fight for so many of the rights our community takes for granted today. It is our duty to make sure they can age with the dignity and respect they deserve. I want to thank Governor Brown for joining our coalition in supporting this bill which will make a real difference in people's lives. The LGBT Senior Bill of Rights is an important step in our fight to ensure all people are treated equal regardless of their sexual orientation or gender identity."[31]

Epilogue

I can't imagine not loving my child for something he cannot control. It is important to love unconditionally, for having a child is about love, not ego.

Get past the stuff.

Get past the prejudiced and disapproving behaviors.

We need to unlearn negative feelings that take us away from God's plan and accept our new normal. God knew I could handle it. He knew that because of my childhood, my career as a nurse, and my goals in life that I would love my "gifts" unconditionally. I have five amazing children and three happen to be gay. He must believe that I am a very special person in his eyes, which is why he entrusted me to love and nurture them unconditionally.

There is a massive and exciting plan for your life, too. He wants to take your entire purpose and fill it with grace so that others will see you as someone unique and wonderful. He wants you make a difference in the world! Allow Him to broaden your vision.

We need to love our children even if they do not fit your definition of normal. We need to accept our new normals. This means fully accepting our children instead of merely tolerating their behavior as some cursed choice. Please embrace, adore, and cherish the gift of parenthood, and don't squander a lifetime of love trying to quash something unquashable.

Each of us has a hero inside of us and a uniqueness that we may not see at first, often because we are so concerned with fitting in. We may have a different way of learning, a different walk, a different talk, a different appearance, and more. You have to learn to celebrate your uniqueness and cherish who you are as a human being. You have to act out of love and compassion for the people in your life and those you come in contact with. Find your inner self, your inner fortitude, and embrace it.

Remember, gay people have lives not lifestyles. People do not change sexual orientation. Marriage is a civil right. And as hard as this is to face, the Bible is being wrongly used to discriminate against the LGBT. Its messages of unconditional love from both God and parents got caught up in misinformed politics somewhere along the way. We need to recapture the emphasis on love and embrace our new normal.

Most of the people that do not understand are caught up with the sexual aspect of being LGBT. Being gay is about love, affection, caring, nurturing, support, trust, and goodness. All those things are factors which make up a healthy relationship. Homosexuality is about how you fall in love. It's how we love that matters. Everyone needs to be loved. The world is a better place when we love well. We need to embrace the total person.

Life is precious, we need to focus on loving one another. Love with your heart, not your mind. The Bible preaches these messages without regard for character. Remember John 13:34, "A new commandment I give unto you, that ye love one another; as I have loved you, that ye also love one another."

Please – the message in this book is important! I urge all mothers and fathers to create a home based on

Love

Acceptance

Mercy

And remember, they are ALWAYS OUR CHILDREN.

Glossary

I felt the need to build a glossary with this book. Many years ago, before I realized that I had gay children, I looked at certain words and their meanings differently. Today, I know that many adults need assistance in understanding vocabulary to help guide them in better understanding our children. Please allow me to clarify certain words and terms that may be uncertain or unclear to you.

Acceptance -   To tolerate without protest, approval, favorable reception, acknowledgment, positive response to someone, willingness to treat someone as part of the group, acknowledging what is true. It does not mean you must compromise your convictions about what constitutes right and wrong, nor does it mean you condone homosexual behavior and practices. Acceptance is showing a deeper level of understanding by treating an LGBT, person as equal.

Stephen Arterburn, best-selling author and respected Christian psychologist, says, "many parents of homosexual children withhold love and affection because they are afraid to appear that they are approving of the gay lifestyle." The truth is that your child needs unconditional love and acceptance more than ever. Withholding love will only make a difficult situation worse. Remember that acceptance is not the same thing as approval.

Bisexual -   Being sexually attracted to both men and women.

<u>Bullying</u> -	Intimidating, mistreating, harassment, maltreatment, single out, discriminate. A person's perceived sexual orientation is the second-most popular reason kids are bullied. The biggest reason is appearance and/or looks.
<u>Coming out</u> -	The arrival of a person or event.
<u>Discrimination</u>-	Single out, victimize, show prejudice elsewhere. Too often, the LGBT face hostility, discrimination and sometimes deadly violence-solely because of their sexual orientation.
<u>Diversity</u> -	Cultural or ethnic variety within a specific, measurable region.
<u>Enthusiasm</u> -	Passion, gusto, zeal, eagerness and interest. Enthusiasm drives progress. A good example is Tom Nobbe, executive director of Gay Games 9, who approached Summit County Council to talk about an Olympic-like event in the Akron-Cleveland area. The Gay Games event have been viewed as one of the biggest amateur sports and cultural festivals in the world, and it's all thanks to Nobbe's enthusiasm.
<u>Faith</u> -	Devotion to or trust in somebody. True loyalty. The mission of faith in America is to educate the public about the harm caused to gay Americans. About half of LGBT adults surveyed (48 %) say they have no religious affiliation, compared with 20% of the general public, according to the Pew Research Center.[23] And those who are religious generally attend worship services less often and attach less importance to their faith than do other religiously affiliated adults. When it comes to religion, the nation's LGBT adults have a unique profile that is less religious than the general population, and as a group they feel religion is unfriendly toward them.

Family -   A group of closely-related people.
                        All families, including yours, have an identifiable
                        structure. It is composed of members / roles (who
                        does what), rules (how each member is supposed
                        to act), power-rankings (who makes and enforces
                        the rules), communication dynamics, alliances and
                        subsystems. A family may have several structures,
                        triggered by regular or special events like child vis-
                        itations, divorces, illnesses, disabilities, geographic
                        moves, financial changes, and other environmental
                        stressors. It is good to focus on family.

Fatherhood -   Often the head of the household. The family's pa-
                        ternal guidance. Although it may have taken a while
                        for fatherhood and acceptance to gel in our house-
                        hold, the fact that my husband, their father, was a
                        great dad speaks volumes! My husband was always
                        involved and always present in their lives.

Gay -   Attracted to the same sex.

Homosexuality -   Attracted to the same sex. Homosexuality is a natural
                        expression of human sexuality.

Judgmental -   To form an opinion, be critical, or to consider. It's up
                        to parents and educators to alter the learning envi-
                        ronment and embed resources of resilience that can
                        help LGBT students feel not only safe, but also re-
                        spected and affirmed.
                        Most of us do not realize the way we judge. Under-
                        standing how we judge others and using empathy
                        and compassion when we judge will improve and en-
                        hance our loving relationships immensely. We tend
                        to judge others in areas where we feel most vulner-
                        able. Judgment kills empathy. And empathy is what
                        builds trust and love. When we feel comfortable with
                        our own imperfections we will stop the need to judge
                        others.

<u>Lesbian</u> -	A homosexual woman.
<u>LGBT</u> -	Lesbian, Gay, Bisexual, and Transgender.
<u>Motherhood</u> -	The maternal guiding force in a household, often seen as a creator, protector, nourisher, founder, and nurturing presence. Perhaps it is not surprising that mothers and their gay sons often describe their relationships as close. Compared to fathers, mothers typically have an advantage because they frequently spend more time with their kids and are seen as more approachable.
<u>Ownership</u> -	Rights, tenure, or possession. The condition of possessing something that is as colorful and diverse as the flags we wave. When you are honest and unapologetic about who you are, you take away the ability of others to define you. You take ownership of who you are.
	It doesn't matter what traits do or do not pertain to you. The growth of a community comes from embracing our differences and viewing each other as equals in our complexities, as individuals in our shared stereotypes. As a group that continues to be met with adversity, prejudice and fear, we should strive to laugh with each other and join hands as much as we can.
<u>Pedophile</u> -	A person with a perverse, sexual desire for children. Homosexuality is not pedophilia. Pedophiles can have a heterosexual, homosexual or bisexual orientation.
<u>Premise</u> -	All family systems exist to fill their member's needs. For example...to nurture. Each family's ability to nurture effectively over time ranges from low to high. One factor that affects a family's nurturance level is how stable and healthy its structure is in.

Pride -
Satisfaction with the self, or having the correct level of respect for the importance and value of your personal character. To obtain personal satisfaction and pleasure in regard to life, efforts, achievements, etc... Source of personal satisfaction.

Cleveland Pride Inc. promotes individuals, organizations and businesses who are willing to practice inclusion; they create long-lasting relationships with the diverse communities in the city of Cleveland and surrounding areas through its annual parade, rallies, and festivals, as well as other activities that increase LGBT and ally visibility.

Rejection -
An act of negativity, denial, or snub to eliminate, discard, or throw out. It can be devastating when someone you love rejects you for any reason, including your sexuality. Rejection due to one's sexuality is one of the main reasons why the LGBT teen suicide rate is so high. Don't become a statistic! People reject others based on their own fear or comfort level.

Respect -
Admiration, value, appreciate, high opinion, esteem, reverence. The greatest single source of resilience for LGBT students in a school may be the presence of supportive adults. Other helpful sources that instill respect may be student clubs that address LGBT student issues (eg. the GSA-Gay Straight Alliance) to offer essential support. These clubs are student-led, usually at the high school or middle school level, and work to address the name-calling, bullying and harassment.

Special -
Extraordinary, distinctive, elite, or superior to others of the same kind.

Straight -
A heterosexual, or being attracted to the opposite sex.

<u>Tolerance</u> -	To permit something; to endure. We tolerate a back ache or tolerate a co-worker that is annoying. The LGBT community is not an annoyance or a negative that needs to be tolerated. In the LGBT context, tolerance is usually synonymous with acceptance.

<u>Trust</u> -	A belief, faith, conviction, confidence, or reliance. Life has many different forks in the road, and we have to have trust ourselves and those we love.
	    "Two roads diverged in the woods and I took
	    the one less traveled by and that has made all
	    the difference." *Robert Frost, poet*
	You must show a tremendous amount of love, trust, and commitment to your gay child.

<u>Unconditional</u> -	Without limitations, unrestricted. If you ever heard the words "I'm gay" from a son or daughter, the truth is that your child needs unconditional love and acceptance from you, their parent.
<u>Unique</u> -	One of a kind, exclusive, exceptional, distinctive, matchless, rare, irreplaceable.
<u>Worry</u> -	A concern, fret, apprehension, to be troubled, agonize. For instance, the LGBT community worries about post-Mandela's South Africa's Constitution guaranteeing equality. I also worry that someone will abuse our gay children. No one deserves abuse!

Parent/Child Contract

Contract With Our LGBT Children

I, _____ , and we, _____the
parents enter into the following contract in order to create a positive and
loving relationship as a family. By agreeing to the terms and conditions of
this family contract, all parties understand and accept that they are bound
by the contract and are not free to vary from the terms and conditions.

YOUR CHILD'S TERMS

I, _____ , agree that I will remain honest and open with my feelings.
I promise to be true to myself, to reach my full potential as a human being
and strive to be successful and passionate about my goals.
I promise to respect you, my parents, and respect myself.
I promise to make health and wellness a priority in my everyday living.
I promise not to take unnecessary risks that could result in my harm or
the harm of others that I care about.
I promise to always make my safety and my well-being a high priority
in all that I do, and I promise to remain on high alert for unexpected
events that may harm me.
I promise to maintain a healthy and happy relationship whether it be
based on a friendship or more.
I will look for loving relationships that will enhance the person I am and
one that will only make my life better and happier than before the relationship developed.

YOUR TERMS

As parents, we promise to communicate and stay open and honest with our feelings and our concerns with a positive attitude.

We promise to work through any dispute with you using positive compromise and negotiation.

We promise to maintain the most important goal which is maintaining a loving and productive relationship with you.

We promise to give you the space you need to become even a better person and adult, knowing when to keep quiet, allowing you time to figure things out.

We promise to give you our full attention when you are trying to convey communication and information to us.

We promise to be good listeners. We promise to remember that listening is key.

We promise to trust your relationship decisions and fully believe that you know what is best to build a fulfilled and happy life for yourself.

We promise to assist you in any way we can in living a happy, well balanced and fulfilled life.

We promise to keep an open door, open heart, and open mind when you make decisions that we do not see eye to eye on.

We promise to accept you for who you are, support you and love you through all of life's ups and downs.

We will remind ourselves that at times it is okay to make mistakes, as long as we analyze it, rise above it, and gain inner strength because of it.

We promise to love you – *unconditionally.*

Both parties acknowledge that this contract is entered into voluntarily and that the terms and conditions will be respected.

Other Resources

These resources are things I've found helpful on my journey. They range from films, to newspapers, to publications, to songs. Please peruse and enjoy!

Windy City Times (LGBT newspaper Chicago)
Own Magazine
Fortunate Family Newsletter
The Living Proof -by Mary J. Blige (*The Help* motion picture)
Anyone and Everyone (Film)
Huffington Post (Liberal American news - NY)
Beyond Acceptance (Heartstone Pictures)
New City Paper - Chicago
Columbus Alive (Columbus Dispatch)
A New Earth - Eckhart Tolle
Aren't They All Our Children by Josh Groban

* * * * *

When God Winks: How The Power Of Coincidence Guides Your Life (Squire Rushnell) – I read the book and felt the message was a good one. It certainly mirrored the message that I wanted to share in this journal.

- See yourself succeeding.
- Cancel negative feelings.
- Deflate your obstacles-wipe away trouble.
- Don't be awestruck by others, instead model them.
- Find a coach.
- Know what your good qualities are.

- Perceive yourself as you wish others perceive you.
- Get the "imp" out of impossible.
- Let Go, Let God.
- Believe in Yourself. Believe that you can be the person you wished you could be.
- Look for God's Winks.

Most of your life's journey, your hands are on the wheel. Don't be afraid to make mistakes, don't make excuses. Be not afraid of life. Believe that life is worth living, your beliefs will help create the fact.

*   *   *   *   *

But, how we respond to life is up to us. We can remain open and confident to move forward. We are a part of the universal plan. We can't lose heart, we need to look for signs and consider what they mean when the signs appear. Become creative and prepared for what comes to you. If you are facing difficult times, what has worked for me:

<u>PAULA'S WINKS</u>

- Let it simmer a bit.
- Let it cool down.
- Take breaks from it. Incubate.
- Distance yourself.
- Be disciplined.
- Decide when you are at your best and where you get your best feelings of self-worth.
- Pay attention to your thoughts and best ideas and act on those that lead you to a positive outcome.
- Rewire your brain to dwell on the positive; negative feelings cause unnecessary happiness.
- Be more thankful.
- Distance yourself from the "Energy Vampires" (negative people).
- Being happy gives off energy.
- Embrace life.

My note about the winks: I hope you never miss your little signs, your winks from God, which are being placed along your path for a reason – even if that reason is no more than a gentle jab, pat on the back or a dose of humor to lift you up. Let's stay hopeful and fully alive.

*   *   *   *   *

I found this basic advice as I researched information for this book. I hope this turns your stumbling blocks into stepping stones and leads you to a path of a happy life, loving parenting and appreciation of the gifts we have been given.

STEPPING STONES

- Gratitude. Everyday be thankful for something
- Get happy. Don't let go of your good mood, it will make your day if you can make someone else's day.
- Pretend people love you, do not enter a room fearing that you will be rejected or criticized. Imagine yourself as Lady Gaga or Ellen DeGeneres walking onto a stage knowing the audience adores you. How you would feel and move at this time will begin your day with love and beauty within?
- Stop worrying about everyone, remember that love and worry are very different.
- Replace worry with something else...praising, hugging, doing good deeds, singing.
- Count on your instincts.
- Trust yourself and recognize what is true.
- Step away from your ego.
- Be nice.
- Only gossip positively! Saying nice things about someone serves as a foundation for emotional survival. Avoid the negative.
- Know when to SHUT UP!
- Parenthood is like a workout: every workout strengthens the muscles. Tackle parenthood with energy and diligence. There will times when we feel as if things are falling apart. We need to stand tall, know who we are, and stand by our truths.
- The most meaningful contribution you can give is love, not money. Caring about other things besides your own happiness brings much reward. Doing something for others can make the difference for you. Feeling as if you have helped someone a sense that you matter. The reward is amazing. The afterglow of the good deed enhances the love of humanity.

*   *   *   *   *

And Tango Makes Three - This book was based on two penguins that became a couple and given an egg to raise. *And Tango Makes Three* is a 2005 children's book written by Peter Parnell and Justin Richardson and illustrated by Henry Cole. The book is based on the true story of Roy and Silo, two male chinstrap penguins in New York's Central Park Zoo. Roy and Silo made a nest together, but they could not have offspring. Mr. Gramsay, the zookeeper gifted them an extra egg from another penguin couple at the zoo. Roy and Silo took turns sitting on the egg and eventually it hatched. The female chick was named "Tango" by the zookeepers.

The book has won many awards, including the ALA Notable Children's Book Nominee in 2006, the ASPCA Henry Bergh Book Award in 2005, and was one of the Bank Street Best Books of the Year in 2006. *And Tango Makes Three* has also been at the center of numerous censorship and culture war debates on same-sex marriage, adoption, and homosexuality in animals. The ALA reports that *And Tango Makes Three* was the most frequently challenged book from 2006 to 2010, except for 2009 when it was the second most frequently challenged.

> *We wrote the book to help parents teach children about same-sex parent families. It's no more an argument in favor of human gay relationships than it is a call for children to swallow their fish whole or sleep on rocks.*
>
> —co-author Justin Richardson, New York Times (2005)[6]

*   *   *   *   *

The Boy Who Grew Flowers - This is a book about a boy who discovers he's different. He lives in shame until he discovers someone else like him. I would recommend this to any parent. Being different doesn't start or end with LGBT.

*   *   *   *   *

The Help - *The Help* is a timeless and universal story about the lines we abide by... and the ones we don't. Wise and observant, the character Abileen would tell anyone that would listen, "You are kind, you are smart, you are important. We need to love our enemies and that is hard to do, but it can start by telling the truth. No one ever asked me what it feels like to be me, once I told the truth about that I felt free. I got to thinking about all people and I knew. Things I have seen and done illustrate to me that you have to be true to who you are. Focus on the *now* in your life."

The Trevor - Founded in 1998 by the creators of the Academy Award winning short film, *Trevor*. The Trevor Project is the leading national organization providing crisis intervention and suicide prevention services to the LGBT community. They assist young people by providing lifesaving and life affirming resources including a nationwide, 24-7 crisis intervention lifeline, digital community and educational programs that create a safe, supportive, and positive environment for everyone. Their vision is a future where the possibilities, opportunities and dreams are the same for all youth regardless of sexual orientation or gender identity.

*   *   *   *   *

P-Flag - Founded in 1972 with a simple act of a mother publicly supporting her gay son, P-Flag is the nation's largest family and ally organization, made up of parents, families, friends and straight allies united with people who are LGBT. P-Flag is committed to advancing equality and societal acceptance of LGBT people through its mission of support, education and advocacy. P-Flag's main focus also is to keep families united. It now has over 350 chapters and 200,000 members and supporters. P-Flag National Headquarters is located in Washington DC. P-Flag promotes the health and well-being of LGBT.

*   *   *   *   *

GSA - The Gay Straight Alliance - GSA are student clubs across the country working to make schools safer and more affirming for students, regardless of sexual orientation or gender identity expression. In 2014, thousands of schools across the country celebrated the 10th anniversary of GLSEN's No Name Calling Week. This has developed into an annual event during which educators emphasize kindness and compassion as a means to eliminate name-calling and bullying of all kinds.

I vote we emphasize and promote this act of kindness and compassion every day not just once a year. One of my son's became very involved and proactive with this club in his high school years ago. Unfortunately, this club was at its earliest development and was not well received or attended. Added bullying acts towards him resulted. In fact, about 9 in 10 LGBT teens have reported being bullied at school within the past year because of their sexual orientation, according to the most recent gay bullying statistics.

The policy at his high school is as follows:

> RELIGIOUS, RACIAL, NATIONAL ORIGIN BIGOTRY AND INTOLERANCE: No student shall display racial, religious or national origin bigotry or intolerance. No student shall violate or urge others to violate the civil rights of any other person.

A nearby school handbook reads:

> The school district is to provide a learning environment for students that is free from hazing, threatening, bullying, cyber bullying, harassment, sexual harassment and intimidation. Students shall not threaten, haze, bully, cyber bully, harass, intimidate or participate in any act, verbal or non-verbal, that injures, degrades, disgraces, or tends to injure, degrade or disgrace any student or school employee. No student shall display racial, religious, or national origin bigotry or intolerance which results in a material or substantial disruption to the school environment or which may reasonably be expected to do so. No student shall violate or urge others to violate the civil rights of any person.

* * * * *

Human Rights Campaign - As the largest civil rights organization working to achieve equality for LGBT Americans, the Human Rights Campaign represents a force of more than one million members and supporters nationwide—all committed to making HRC's vision a reality. Founded in 1980, HRC advocates on behalf of LGBT Americans, mobilizes grassroots actions in diverse communities, invests strategically to elect fair-minded individuals to office and educates the public about LGBT issues.

Acknowledgements

My Heartfelt Thanks!

To my support team:

Chicago
Marko, Paul, Tommy, Joey, and Mike; Hadley Rue

Columbus
Drew, Casey, and Robin

To the friends that enhanced the information for this book
and helped me learn and understand.

And most importantly, my husband and my five children!

* * * * *

I had a great deal more people I wanted to acknowledge, and in more depth, too! The following pages list people who were inspirational in my personal life, research, or during the creative process in writing this book.

THE FAMOUS, THE FABULOUS AND THE INSPIRATIONAL

<u>Father John</u> - Led the "Always Our Children" Support Group.

<u>Sr. Rita</u> - Backbone and leader of all the support groups in the NE Ohio area.

<u>Ellen DeGeneres</u> - Has given me much inspiration and energy to write on this topic.

<u>Lady Gaga</u> - Dedicated, strong and passionate advocate for the LGBT community.

<u>Father Pilla</u> - He introduced the support groups to Cleveland.

<u>Tracy Baim</u> - Writer and editor by trade—someone that believed in me and the cause.

<u>Mel Horvath Cockerill</u> - True and loyal friend to my Anthony.

<u>Jane Toma</u> - My publisher and the expert that brought the project to completion.

<u>Jeremy Jusek</u> - My editor and cheerleader. From the very beginning he believed in my book's mission and purpose!

<u>Jared Leto</u> - The Oscar Winner in 2014 for *The Dallas Buyers Club*. His acceptance speech was outstanding:

> *To all the dreamers out there around the world watching this tonight in places like Ukraine and Venezuela, I want to say we are here and as you struggle to make your dreams happen and live the impossible, we are thinking of you tonight."*
> *To follow, he recognized many people with gratitude...before he finished he added these wonderful words of inspiration...*
> *This is for the 36 million people who have lost the battle to AIDS. And to those of you who have ever felt injustice because of who you are and who you love. I stand here in front of the world with you and for you.*

<u>Michael Bishop</u> - Age 40, from Columbus, Ohio. I was very happy to inteview him and hear his story. Here is what he had to say:

> "I don't remember the first time I got drunk." That's how he began our first conversation. "But, I do remember sneaking beers when I was in junior high and high school—I started sneaking into bars at age 19. I was drinking with strangers and trying to figure my life out. Growing up in the 1990's as a gay teen was very different than it is now. My family did not acknowledge it. Homosexuality was not accepted. So the only way to be around people that were similar to me was to visit bars.

"Being gay was not an immediate problem for me but the combination of underage drinking and being gay became an issue for me. I felt the need to drink to fit in. I was desperate to form an identity and understand who I was. I achieved the exact opposite as I drank heavily and made poor decisions. I couldn't seem to form any solid personal relationships... or solid friendships for that matter.

"As time continued, addiction set in and my relationships turned to others with addictions. I was able to realize that I was headed down a dangerous path. I discovered that my best friend was me. Being completely honest with myself and others was the beginning of recovery.

"In 2010, I woke up in an Intensive Care Unit and was unsure how I got there. I did not want to die alone, something clicked, until then I never really cared about myself or who I was. I had many teachable moments and knew I needed to change my world.

"There is a reason I survived that hospitalization. The reason I am alive today and the reason things happened to me has made me who I am today. I wouldn't have the wonderful people in my life without the past. Since that time, I still visit the same bars but my visits are different. Perhaps my conversation with someone will make their life better. As I socialize and open up to the people around me, I admit to them that I don't drink. I am open and honest about my life and my history. When someone asks why, I tell them. I find that the people in the LGBT community are most supportive in so many ways. We truly are a close community. It makes me feel good to make people feel good about themselves, stronger about themselves and better than before. I always tell people, 'it starts with liking yourself.' "

Josh McKinley - One of the best track athletes in our hometown, he has gained fame as a fashion designer and a reality TV star on the show Project Runway. "Your sexuality has nothing to do with how well you perform on the track, field or court," he said, "it's all about overcoming obstacles and pushing forward."

Jeanne Manford - Marched with her son in 1972 in New York's Liberation Parade. During this parade many gay and lesbian people ran up to Jeanne during the parade and begged her to talk to their parents, so she decided to begin a support group.

Michael Sam - Sam came out publicly on 2/9/14 to the *New York Times* and *ESPN* as gay. Sam was a draft pick for an NFL Team. He was the first openly gay NFL player. We finally got to see that a player's sexual orientation has nothing to do with his ability to excel on the football field. "I just want to make sure I could tell my story the way I want to tell it. I just want to own the truth." Sam told the *NYTimes*.

Daniela - Daniela was struggling with the truth. She was scared to tell her parents that she was struggling with her sexual identity. She was on Dr. Phil, who asked her "Daniela, what do you want from your parents?" Her immediate response was "acceptance." Her parents admitted that Daniella has been struggling with her identity especially since her father admits to using homophobic slurs in the past.

But her father said he loves his daughter no matter what. He realized that his words hurt her feelings. "It's verbally abusive and she probably heard those slurs her entire life." The moment was heartfelt. Her father also said "I feel like an #&%."

Dr. Phil then pointed at Daniella's parents sternly. "It is a hard life living a lie every day of your existence. That's a hard life."

Miriam Ben-Shalom - Born May 3, 1948, She was an American educator, activist and former staff sergeant in the United States Army. After being discharged from the military for homosexuality in 1976, she successfully challenged her discharge in court and returned to military service in 1987. She is the first openly gay or lesbian to be reinstated after being discharged under the military's policy excluding homosexuals from military service. She served until 1990 when the Army succeeded in terminating her service after prolonged judicial proceedings.

Chely Wright - She is an American country music artist and gay rights activist that, according to *Windy City Times*, was one of the first major country music performers to step out of the closet in 2010.

Born in 1970 in Kansas City, Missouri realized at age 8 that she was gay. She is known for her songs "Shut Up and Drive" and "Single White Female" (1999). She was a grand marshall in the Phoenix Pride Parade. She harbored the belief that her sexual orientation would kill her career, so she resolved to never confide her orientation to anyone or pursue romantic relationships with women.

As a songwriter she has written songs recorded by Brad Paisley, Clay Walker, Indigo Girls and Richard Marx. While touring with Brad Paisley in 2000 she began an affair with him. She stated that she never had the capacity to fall in love with him but had a sexual attraction to him. She held Brad in high esteem and had great affection for him in every way. She expressed remorse for how she treated him. She admitted to Oprah Winfrey that, "I have a lot of regret for how that relationship began and ended. I had no business being in a relationship with him."

She claims she came out to free herself from the burdens of living a lie, to lend support to gay children and teens, and to counter the belief that gays are wicked and defective. In 2010, Wright founded her second charity, the "Like Me" organization. This organization provides assistance, resources, and education to LGBT individuals and their family and friends.

In August 2011 Wright married Lauren Blitzer, LGBT rights advocate in Connecticut. Her two reasons for "coming out " were her strong concerns about bullying and hate crimes towards gays, particularly gay teens." Her second reason was in regard to the damage to her life caused by "lying and hiding."

Joe Bell - Joe Bell walked for a very long time. He walked from Oregon to New York City where his 15-year-old son Jadin had always wanted to live. Jadin committed suicide earlier that year after being bullied at school for being gay.

After the suicide, Bell promptly quit his job and walked, stopping only for schools along the way to offer support to struggling teens and to convey to bullies that the pain they cause is long term. Bell tells teens that once they are out of school there is so much more to live for.

Steve Grand - Born in 1990, is an American musician and singer-songwriter from Lemont, Illinois. He became an internet celebrity and was acclaimed by many as the first openly gay male country singer to attract mainstream attention in the US. He is famous for his music video "All American Boy." This video went viral in July 2013.

Grand wrote music from the time he was 11. He knew he was gay at age 13 and struggled to reconcile his sexuality with his Catholic faith. He came out to his friends while in the 8th grade. After his parents learned of his sexuality they enrolled him in psychotherapy for five years. Some called it conversion therapy and his therapist tried to convince him that he would be happier if he didn't live the life of a gay man.

Although he decided the therapy was ineffective he has expressed his gratitude toward his therapist. "He believed in me and was compassionate." Steve was able to recognize at the time that homosexuality was not a bad thing or sinful and not something that God wants you to rid yourself of. Grand has faced much criticism because he has declined to condemn conversion therapy. He also continued his career as the music director at his Catholic church. He has drawn criticism from activists who question whether he can be viewed as a positive role model.

Harvey Milk - Harvey Hay founded the Matachine Society, the First American Gay Rights Group. The first meeting was held in Los Angeles, California in 1950. By 1953, there were over 2,000 members. He established one of the first gay newspapers, *The Call-One*. The movie, "Milk" is informative and inspiring portrayal of his life.

He spoke to many in the LGBT community, always with incredibly kind words. He was known for saying phrases like "I am here to recruit you. You don't need fixed, there is nothing wrong with you. God does not hate you, you are not wrong, you are not sick. It's about hope, about the 'us,' without hope the *us* gives up! Life is not worth living without hope. It's about the family not about the power, or the ego or about the personal gain. Destroy every closet door."

Harvey also said "We feel there is power in sexuality because our culture is so afraid of us. If you're going to carry the skin of conformity over you, you are going to suppress the beautiful prince or princes within you."

His words are inspiring, and he also emphasized diversity in his speeches. "Are you reactive or proactive? Many men want to be respected as human beings and they don't want to live on edge. Get to know your child, show an interest even if you aren't. We have to give our kids hope! Deep inside they are different and unique and looking for acceptance in the world, in their families and in their environment. Hope is alive! Destroy every closet door! It's not about the ego! All deserve a chance! Be kind, be sensitive!" It's not about black/white, Asian, senior citizens, the disabled, gay, straight, it's about life for a better tomorrow!"

Nelson Mandela - His life was full of suffering and hardships that led him to be a caring and compassionate leader of South Africa. The seven principles that he used to become a renowned leader are:

- He Anticipated
- He Challenged
- He Interpreted
- He Decided
- He Aligned
- He Learned
- He Shaped [the future with equality]

Miriam Hoover - A charitable hero of Chicago's LGBT scene who died recently at the age of 104. Her work helped fund dozens of artistic projects and nonprofit organizations in the city, including the Chicago House, the Hoover-Leppen Theater at the Center on Halsted, the Bonaventure House, the Art Institute of Chicago, the Chicago Symphony Orchestra, and various AIDS organizations.

With the help of her philanthropist nephew Michael, she was an active member in the LGBT community and avid promoter of gay rights. She is the first female Canon elected to St. James Cathedral in Chicago and she received an honorary doctorate from Seabury Western Theological Seminary. Her and her husband also received a star on the walk in Palm Springs and the Steve Chase Humanitarian award from Desert AIDS Project.

Bibliography

[1] Liptak, Adam. "Supreme Court Ruling Makes Same-Sex Marriage a Right Nationwide." *NYTimes*. 26 June, 2015. https://www.nytimes.com/2015/06/27/us/supreme-court-same-sex-marriage.html

[2] " 'I've known you were gay since you were six, I've loved you since you were born': Dad's touching letter accepting gay son goes viral" *Daily Mail*. 16 March 2013. http://www.dailymail.co.uk/news/article-2294281/Dads-touching-letter-accepting-gay-son-goes-viral.html

[3] Seaton, Jaimie. "Homeless rates for LGBT teens are alarming, but parents can make a difference." *The Washington Post*. 29 March 2017. https://www.washingtonpost.com/news/parenting/wp/2017/03/29/homeless-rates-for-lgbt-teens-are-alarming-heres-how-parents-can-change-that/?utm_term=.9285a37f71b8

[4] Balter, Michael. "Homosexuality may be caused by chemical modifications to DNA." *Science Magazine*. 8 Oct 2015. http://www.sciencemag.org/news/2015/10/homosexuality-may-be-caused-chemical-modifications-dna

[5] Rahman, Qazi. " 'Gay genes': science is on the right track, we're born this way. Let's deal with it." *The Guardian*. 24 July 2015. https://www.theguardian.com/science/blog/2015/jul/24/gay-genes-science-is-on-the-right-track-were-born-this-way-lets-deal-with-it

[6] Meyer, Ilan H. "Prejudice, Social Stress, and Mental Health in Lesbian, Gay, and Bisexual Populations: Conceptual Issues and Research Evidence." *National Center for Biotechnology Information.* PMC 9 Nov 2007. Published in final edited form as: Psycho Bull. 2003 Sept; 129(5), pp 674-697. https://www.ncbi.nlm.nih.gov/pmc/articles/PMC2072932/

[7] Robison, Jennifer. "What Percentage of the Population is Gay?" *Gallup.* 8 Oct 2002. http://news.gallup.com/poll/6961/what-percentage-population-gay.aspx

[8] Gates, Gary J. "In U.S., More Adults Identifying as LGBT" *Gallup.* 11 Jan 2017. http://news.gallup.com/poll/201731/lgbt-identification-rises.aspx

[9] "Growing Up LGBT in America" *Human Rights Campaign.* n.d. https://www.hrc.org/youth-report/view-and-share-statistics

[10] Kann L, Olsen EO, McManus T, et al. "Sexual Identity, Sex of Sexual Contacts, and Health-Related Behaviors Among Students in Grades 9-12 – United States and Selected Sites" *MMWR Surveill Summ* 2016; 65(9): 1-202.

[11] Drescher, Jack. "Out of DSM: Depathologizing Homosexuality" *US National Library of Medicine, National Institutes of Health.* Dec 2015; v5(4): 565-575. https://www.ncbi.nlm.nih.gov/pmc/articles/PMC4695779/

[12] Anton, B. S. (2010). Proceedings of the American Psychological Association for the legislative year 2009: Minutes of the annual meeting of the Council of Representatives and minutes of the meetings of the Board of Directors. *American Psychologist*, 65, 385–475. doi:10.1037/a0019553 <http://www.apa.org/about/policy/sexual-orientation.pdf>

[13] Neroulias, Nicole. "Washington state's governor signs gay marriage law." *Reuters.* 13 Feb 2012. https://www.reuters.com/article/us-gay-marriage-washington/washington-states-governor-signs-gay-marriage-law-idUSTRE81C15L20120213

[14] Schwartz, John. "Highlights From the Supreme Court Decision on Same-Sex Marriage" *NYTimes.* 8 June 2015. https://www.nytimes.com/interactive/2015/us/2014-term-supreme-court-decision-same-sex-marriage.html

[15] Eckholm, Erik. "The Same-Sex Couple Who Got a Marriage License in 1971" *NYTimes*. 16 May 2015. https://www.nytimes.com/2015/05/17/us/the-same-sex-couple-who-got-a-marriage-license-in-1971.html

[16] Sant'Ambrogio, Michael D. "*Baehr v. Lewin* and the Long Road to Marriage Equality" *Michigan State University College of Law*. 2011. https://digitalcommons.law.msu.edu/cgi/viewcontent.cgi?article=1523&context=facpubs

[17] Reilly, Ryan J; Siddiqui, Sabrina. "Supreme Court DOMA Decision Rules Federal Same-Sex Marriage Ban Unconstitutional" *HuffPost*. 26 June 2013. https://www.huffingtonpost.com/2013/06/26/supreme-court-doma-decision_n_3454811.html

[18] Herek, Gregory M. "Stigma and Sexual Orientation: Understanding Prejudice Against Lesbians, Gay Men, and Bisexuals" *University of Virginia*. 21 May 2008. Print. 278 pgs.

[19] Gates, Gary J. "Lesbian, gay, and bisexual men and women in the US military: Updated estimates." *The Williams Institute*. May 2010. https://williamsinstitute.law.ucla.edu/wp-content/uploads/Gates-GLBmilitaryUpdate-May-20101.pdf

[20] Ryan, Caitlin. *The Family Acceptance Project*. https://familyproject.sfsu.edu/

[21] "Sexual Identity, Sex of Sexual Contacts, and Health-Related Behaviors Among Students in Grades 9-12 — United States and Selected Sites, 2015" *Surveillance Summaries Morbidity and Mortality Weekly Report* Vol. 65, No. 9, 12 August 2016. CDC. https://www.cdc.gov/mmwr/volumes/65/ss/pdfs/ss6509.pdf

[22] "Changing Attitudes on Gay Marriage" *Pew Research Center*. 26 June 2017. Pew Fact Sheet. http://www.pewforum.org/fact-sheet/changing-attitudes-on-gay-marriage/

[23] Murphy, Caryle. "Lesbian, gay and bisexual Americans differ from general public in their religious affiliations" *Pew Research Center.* 26 May 2015. http://www.pewresearch.org/fact-tank/2015/05/26/lesbian-gay-and-bisexual-americans-differ-from-general-public-in-their-religious-affiliations/

[24] Bilodeau, Brent L.; Renn, Kristen A. "Analysis of LGBT Identity Development Models and Implications for Practice" *Michigan State University.* n.d. https://msu.edu/~renn/BilodeauRennNDSS.pdf

[25] Koebler, Jason. "Scientists May Have Finally Unlocked Puzzle of Why People Are Gay" *US News.* 11 Dec 2012. https://www.usnews.com/news/articles/2012/12/11/scientists-may-have-finally-unlocked-puzzle-of-why-people-are-gay

[26] Jeong, Josiah. "1,500 Animal Species Practice Homosexuality" *News Medical.* 23 October 2006. https://www.news-medical.net/news/2006/10/23/1500-animal-species-practice-homosexuality.aspx

[27] Thorpe, JR. "A Brief History of Bisexuality, From Ancient Greece and the Kinsey Scale to Lindsay Lohan" 23 Sept 2014. https://www.bustle.com/articles/40282-a-brief-history-of-bisexuality-from-ancient-greece-and-the-kinsey-scale-to-lindsay-lohan

[28] http://vistriai.com/kinseyscaletest/

[29] Sorrell, Stephanie. "Depression as a Spiritual Journey" *John Hunt Publishing Ltd.* 2009. Print.

[30] Kang, Dake. "Response to Flyer Urging LGBT Students to Kill Themselves Was 'Inadequate,' College Says" *Yahoo.* 21 October 2017. https://www.yahoo.com/news/response-flyer-urging-lgbt-students-165502048.html

[31] Hagstrom, Anders. "California Can Now Jail People For Misusing Gender Pronouns" *Daily Caller.* 6 October 2017. http://dailycaller.com/2017/10/06/california-can-now-jail-people-for-misusing-gender-pronouns/